The Poles in Oklahoma

by Richard M. Bernard

For Jim —
Thanks for
taking all the Duncan
pressure off
of me for all
these years —

Dick
X-mas
1980

Oklahoma Image is a project sponsored by the Oklahoma Department of Libraries and the Oklahoma Library Association, and made possible by a grant from the National Endowment for the Humanities.

CONTENTS

To Elizabeth Cole Bernard

PREFACE

The history of the Polish people of Oklahoma is a story of hard work and struggle to carve out new lives in a new land. Most Poles who came to the present state of Oklahoma had suffered hardships in a European homeland dominated by hostile neighbors. From Prussian-, Russian-, and Austrian-Poland, they came by the hundreds of thousands to America with some of their numbers eventually settling on the last American frontier in Oklahoma. Most came as rural peasants but became miners, farmers, and smelter workers. Others who came later, along with the sons and daughters of the first to arrive, became businessmen and professionals, shopkeepers, lawyers, priests, and nuns. More recently, some have risen to high positions in the governmental and educational structures of the state.

Not many Oklahomans know the story of the Polish people of the Sooner State. The Poles of Oklahoma have not left a very easy trail to follow. They were never more than 4,000 in number according to U.S. census counts. And, most Poles who lived in the state at one time or another eventually departed, leaving behind few traces of their sojourn in the area. Those who did remain left few written documents, the sort of material that most historians use. Fewer still of these materials have found places in the standard historical depositories of the state. This loss of information is tragic for such materials cannot be replaced. Indeed, there is fear today in the state's largest Polish community at Harrah that an entire heritage may be lost before parents, churches, and schools can transmit its values to a younger generation.

The best hope for recovering the Polish-Oklahoman heritage, therefore, lies in oral accounts of times past. Fortunately, there are still Polish people in Oklahoma who can recall territorial days as well as others who can report much about more recent Polish experiences. With their help, and that of other scholars, archivists, and librarians, and through use of the few remaining written materials, the author has been able to produce this account. He is very grateful indeed to the many people with whom he has talked and corresponded.

The following people supplied material and advice useful for Chapter One of this book: Professor Douglas P. Hale (Oklahoma State University, Stillwater), Sister Mary Dolores, C.S.S.F., (Okarche Memorial Hospital), Sister Mary Frances Hopcus, C.S.S.F., (Bishop McGuinness High School, Oklahoma City), Sister Rosemarie, C.S.S.F., (Rio Rancho, N. Mex.), Professor Joe Hubbell (Southwestern State

University, Weatherford), Professor Bill Snodgrass (Phillips University, Enid), Mrs. Gertrude Kosmoski Sterba (Ponca City), Mr. Jim Olzawski (Jenks), and the following librarians: Mr. Larry Thorne (Alva), Ms. Georgie Throckmorton (Enid), Ms. Edna Conley (Pawhuska), and Ms. Yvette M. Kolstrom (Lawton). Some of the material used in Chapter Two came from: Mrs. Clementine Gornik, Mr. Andrew Waitrovich, Jr., and Father Martin Morgan (Hartshorne), Mrs. Michalina Sokolosky, Mr. and Mrs. Julian Shamasko and Father H. J. Foken (McAlester), and Mr. C. G. Fultz and Mr. Richard Reed (Gowen).

Those who assisted in the preparation of Chapter Three include the following from Harrah: Mrs. Lillie Bradley, Mr. John L. Hopcus, Mrs. Martha Hopcus, Mr. and Mrs. Raymond Hopcus, Mr. Frank Kusek, Mr. Leo "Bud" Kusek, Mrs. Selena Kusek, Mrs. Frances Magott, Father Gerard Nathe, O.S.B., Mrs. Mary Nowakowski, Mr. Dan Senkowski, and Ms. Donna Wyskup. Others read and corrected an earlier version of this chapter. They were Father Eugene Marshall, O.S.B., Sister Mary Frances Hopcus, C.S.S.F., (as noted), and Mrs. Elizabeth C. Bernard and Mr. G. C. Bowman (Duncan).

Mr. Stanley Kazmierzak of Bartlesville spent many long hours collecting much of the material in Chapter Four. For several years, he has gathered data on the Polish people of that city, and since August 1978, he has also assisted in tracking down specific bits of information. That chapter is in fact a tribute to his perseverance and his desire to make known the Polish heritage of his hometown. Others helped on the chapter also. These include Mr. Martin I. Zofness, Father Lee O'Neil and Mr. Joe Barber of Bartlesville, and archivists James E. Van Houten (U.S. Census Bureau, Pittsburg, Kan.), Ruby Cranor (Bartlesville), and Bradford Koplowitz (State Archives, Oklahoma City).

Several of the priests mentioned in Chapter Five supplied information and proofread early versions of the work. These include the Rt. Rev. Monsignor Antoni F. Chojecki and Father Marek Maszkiewicz (St. John's Medical Center, Tulsa), Fathers Wenceslaus L. Karas and John Schug, O.F.M., Cap. (St. Anne's Friary, Broken Arrow), Father Alojzy Waleczak (Our Lady of Mercy, Jersey City, N.J.), and Father David F. Monahan (The *Sooner Catholic*, Oklahoma City).

The author wishes to thank all of these people for their help. He also greatly appreciates the help of Professors H. Wayne Morgan, Rennard Strickland, and Douglas P. Hale; Mrs. Janet Black and Mrs. Terry L. Bernard in preparing the manuscript. This has by no means been a one-person project.

Marquette University   *Richard M. Bernard*

Chapter 1

NEWCOMERS TO A NEW LAND

Although rounded and smoothed by centuries of wind erosion, the ancient Wichita Mountains of southwestern Oklahoma still rise in scenic contrast to the flat, dry range lands that surround them. From the modern city of Lawton, they stretch north and west across Comanche County and push into the lower two-thirds of Kiowa County, near Hobart. Together mountains and range form a quiet western setting which to the Anglo-American has but one unusual element. Near the southern edge of the Wichitas is a small, granite mountain with a name more reminiscent of faraway eastern Europe than of anywhere else on the Great Plains. It is Mount Radziminski, a natural monument to the first Polish immigrant to make his mark on Oklahoma history.

Charles Radziminski, a civil engineer and surveyor, may have been the first Pole to leave his name on the history of the Sooner State. He was certainly not the last, for within fifty years of his untimely death in 1858, hundreds of Polish people had migrated to Oklahoma to make new homes in this new land. He came to this country from an occupied Poland, under the tripartite rule of Prussia, Russia, and Austria. As a twenty-five-year-old lieutenant in the rebellious Polish army, he fought against his country's Russian masters in an unsuccessful revolt in 1830–31. His unit fled from the homeland in the fall of 1831, and he crossed the Austrian border only to fall into the hands of Viennese authorities. Although as a standard practice the Austrians captured and returned enlisted men to the Czarist regime, they allowed officers to choose voluntary exile abroad. Thus, in 1834, Charles Radziminski and nearly three hundred other officers sailed for America where he found work in Virginia as a civil engineer.

A decade after his arrival, Charles Radziminski joined the U.S. Army and served in the Mexican War as a second lieutenant in the

1

Third Regiment, U. S. Dragoons. After hostilities ended, he remained in the military as a surveyor. He assisted in drawing the Maine–New Brunswick boundary, as the Webster-Ashburton Treaty authorized, and later obtained an appointment to the joint U.S.–Mexican Boundary Commission. As surveyor, then secretary, to this group, he helped set the international border from the Rio Grande to the Pacific.

Promoted to first lieutenant, Radziminski then joined "Jeff Davis' Own" Second Cavalry, created by the Mississippian when he was secretary of war. Stationed on the Texas frontier, this regiment protected white settlers against Indian raids. Radziminski remained with this outfit until 1858, when his health began to fail. "Consumption" (tuberculosis) finally forced him to give up his duties. Having no relatives or close friends in America, he used his life savings to check into one of Memphis, Tennessee's most fashionable hotels in July of that year, and died there a month later.

Soon after his death, several companies of his Second Cavalry Regiment, supported by infantry and Indian scouts, established a new outpost north of the Red River. Brevet Major Earl Van Dorn, the commanding officer, named the new installation Camp Radziminski in honor of the Polish lieutenant. Although moved twice, Camp Radziminski became the base for military operations against the Comanches at Wichita Village, near Rush Springs. Not far from the site of the old encampment, located four miles northwest of Mountain Park in Kiowa County, stands the mountain of the same name. Though not recognized on official state maps, Mount Radziminski remains well known to area residents.[1]

Radziminski and other Poles who came to this country before the 1880s were the first gentle waves of a migration that crested at flood level in the years before World War I. At most, no more than 50,000 Poles had arrived in the United States before 1870 and in the decade that followed, an average of only 1,100 people debarked annually. That yearly average grew to nearly 10,000 in the 1880s and to roughly 12,000 in the nineties. Then, between 1897 and 1913, over two million Polish people landed on American shores. In 1880, only 48,557 Polish-born people lived in the United States. By the turn of the century, that figure had risen to 383,407; and by 1920 it was over a million. When the 1920 census officials combined these people with their American-born children, they discovered nearly 2.4 million individuals of "Polish-stock" residing in this country.[2]

Since 1795, these Poles and the thousands of others who never left Europe, had been without an independent fatherland. In that year, Poland's military-minded neighbors, Prussia, Russia, and Austria, had completed the last of three partitions of the old Polish state. For over a century thereafter, until the Treaty of Versailles officially ended the Great War, Poles labored under foreign taskmasters, a situation that encouraged many Polish people to seek new opportunities abroad.

During the 1870s, the greatest out-migration of Poles originated in the German-held provinces where the total outflow surpassed 150,000 people. The numbers of German migrants, however, soon fell behind those from Galicia (Austrian Poland), and during the 1880s, more people left that sector than any other. From the turn of the century to the outbreak of World War I, the Russian-occupied region surrendered slightly more migrants than either of the more western areas. In this last period, some 370,000 Russian Poles left their homeland, compared to about 336,000 Galicians and only 32,000 German Poles.[3]

Historically an agricultural area, Prussian Poland suffered terribly from poor harvests in 1848 and 1853–56, years when crop production was up elsewhere. Thus, Polish farmers felt the double blow of low output and low prices for their farm products. By the late 1850s it was clear that only large financial investments could revive the area's economy. In 1858, Prussian Prime Minister Otto von Bismarck interceded and established a land bank to facilitate real-estate sales to German buyers. Such men brought new capital to the region, but their presence also hastened "Prussianization" and reduced still further the standard of living of the Polish peasants.

These newcomers had little sympathy for the Polish people who had worked the land for centuries. As landlords and employers, their primary concern was reducing the cost of labor. They sent to the Austrian- and Russian-held provinces for field hands who quickly flooded local labor markets and resulted in lower wages for everyone. This action alone probably accounted for the great bulk of the emigration from German Poland in the 1870s and 1880s. Other causes included Bismarck's attacks on the Catholic church and on Polish culture (his *Kulturkampf*) and the ever-present threat of compulsory military service.

Galicia was even poorer than German Poland. Although comparatively liberal in matters of politics, religion, and culture, the Viennese government maintained a mercantilist attitude toward the economy of its Polish territory. Galicia was, in effect, a colony, the breadbasket for the Hapsburg empire. While Austria proper industrialized, government officials discouraged the introduction of machinery

3

and factories in the empire's northern outposts. This action met little opposition from the Polish gentry, the *szlachta,* who also sought to keep peasants on the land in order to prevent agricultural labor shortages and accompanying wage hikes. Left as a farming colony, Galicia suffered through one depression after another in the late nineteenth and early twentieth centuries. It was from these economic plagues that many Poles fled to the American "promised land."

In Congress Poland, the Russian sector, the situation proved more complex, but yielded similar results. Although the Russians had followed Austria's example and abolished serfdom in 1864, they still kept a tight grip over Polish politics, education, and religion. Their economic planning, in fact, was quite comprehensive and called for modern diversification within their Polish territories. Czarist officials kept the northern provinces agricultural, but allowed factories to develop elsewhere in cities such as Lodz and Czestochowa.

Despite these best laid plans, agricultural downturns in the north in the late nineteenth century resulted in substantial emigration. Before 1904 more people left from that area than from any other in Congress Poland. The following year brought an end to the ill-fated Russo-Japanese War, and with peace came a postwar depression and industrial strife. Hardest hit were the industrial cities from which many fled for lack of employment. A large number of these sailed for America; so many, in fact, that by 1908, factory hands comprised the majority of emigrants from the Russian sector.

Despite the departures of these workers, most Polish emigrants were peasant farmers and were among the poorest people in all of Europe. Typically they and their families shared two-room huts with their farm livestock. They wore simple cotton and sheepskin clothing, and ate plain, staple food such as potatoes, cabbage, beets, and beans. Meat was a rare holiday fare.[4]

Day to day hardships, however, proved less threatening in the long run than the unseen workings of the "demographic squeeze." The problem was simple: too many people tried to earn their livings on too little land. At the time, Catholic Poland had one of the world's highest birth rates. That fact, coupled with a falling death rate, meant that total population figures soared. In Russian Poland, for example, there were twice as many people (over 10 million) in 1900 as there had been a quarter of a century earlier.[5]

The Polish peasant, who viewed himself as the caretaker of ancestral property, had less and less to supervise. Keeping with ancient traditions, peasant fathers attempted to leave at least a part of their land to each male offspring. Over the years, however, the system became less feasible. Ultimately, these repeated subdivisions pushed the size of the average family farm below that necessary for mere survival. Unable to support themselves, let alone wives and children, many Polish men gave up the independence of farm operation and sought work as migrant laborers on the large estates of central Europe. Many others, along with a number of women and youngsters, boarded ships for America.

Who could blame them? In Galicia, farm wages averaged twelve cents per day, only about one-eighth that of agricultural workers in the U.S. American factory hands earned twelve times what Polish laborers made. Even factory workers in the rapidly growing cities of Russian Poland could quadruple their wages in the American promised land. Many heard these figures, and most sailed with the intention of earning their fortunes and returning triumphantly to Polish soil. Few, however, came back in that manner.[6]

Polish people came to this country ready and willing to work, and in demographic terms, they had great earning potential. Few were either too young or too old to find steady employment. Fully 90 percent of these newcomers were in their most productive years between the ages of 14 and 44. And in an age when male wages stood far above those for women, Polish males outnumbered Polish females by roughly two to one.[7]

In terms of marketable skills, however, few of these men and women had the credentials to secure well-paying positions. Over 90 percent of the newcomers who even listed an occupation referred to themselves as "laborers" or "farm laborers." Many simply gave no occupation at all.[8] Had these peasant peoples arrived in an earlier, more agricultural era, they would have found great farming opportunities for those able to purchase some of this country's relatively cheap virgin lands. These newcomers, however, confronted an urbanized, industrial America where most farmers had difficulty earning enough money and where new ones found life on the soil all but impossible. For the vast majority of these immigrants, the agricultural skills of the Old World proved useless as most Poles became factory hands and common laborers.

Hundreds of thousands of Polish people poured into the states of the industrial Northeast and Midwest, but thousands of others scattered across every region of the nation, except the South. Quite a number found new homes in the Great Plains states stretching northward from Texas to Nebraska.[9] Panna Maria, Texas, founded

The Poles in Oklahoma

in 1854 and named after the Virgin Mary, claims to be the country's oldest Polish settlement.[10] The Lone Star and Cornhusker states each had roughly 25,000 Poles by 1919, while the Jayhawkers of Kansas counted about half that number in their midst. By 1910, about 1,300 Polish-born immigrants and their families had made their homes in Oklahoma.[11]

GRAPH 1

Oklahoma's Polish People
1890 - 1970

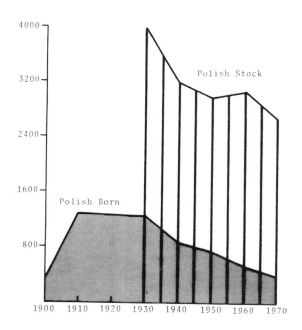

Source: U. S. Censuses

Aside from Lieutenant Radziminski, a handful of coal miners represented the earliest Polish arrivals within the current boundaries of the Sooner State. Mining companies, which began operations in Indian Territory in 1873, brought the first Polish laborers to the McAlester District three years later. This area, the heart of which extended through Pittsburg and Latimer Counties, between McAlester and Wilburton, continued to attract Poles as long as the mines prospered. The 1900 census listed 109 Polish miners in Indian Territory with nearly all of them in that one district.[12]

Only a few Polish people, however, joined in the Run of April 22, 1889, which opened the Unassigned Lands to white settlement. In fact, fourteen months later, the census taker could have counted on one hand the number of Poles residing in the new Oklahoma Territory.

Among them was fifty-seven-year-old Lawrence Mikolajyagck, who came to Oklahoma City with his daughter and son-in-law about the time of the run itself. Annie Mikolajyagck Ambroz, like her father, had migrated to America from Poland. She had married Joseph Ambroz, a Bohemian by birth, who may have been Polish also. All three had lived in this country for a number of years, and the men had become American citizens. The Mikolajyagck-Ambroz family came to Oklahoma from Nebraska where the two Ambroz children, Adolph and William, had been born.[13]

Fifty-year-old Robert Aniol, on the other hand, immigrated from Poland to Texas. Shortly after the Run, he and his Michigan-born wife Bridgett brought their three sons to the wilds of Cleveland County. Charles Liebler, a native of the old country, and his wife and son also settled in Canadian County in the late spring of 1889. These four foreign-born pioneers represented the sum total of Polonia in Oklahoma Territory in 1890.

No more than two years passed, however, before the founding of a Polish farming community at Harrah, the only one of its kind in either of the Twin Territories. Located on what became the eastern edge of Oklahoma County, the Harrah settlement began on Indian lands made available to whites in 1891. Within months of the land run that opened the area on September 22 of that year, ten Polish families came from Marche, Arkansas. Although by 1900, their numbers had grown to only fourteen families, many others followed in the early twentieth century. Today, several hundred people of Polish extraction live in that community or in others nearby.[14]

Shortly after Oklahoma obtained statehood in 1907, other Polish people migrated to Bartlesville, hoping to find employment in the newly built zinc smelters of that city. Other Poles provided services to these working men and their families, and soon grocery clerks and shopkeepers were conducting business in the Polish language. That city's Polish population of immigrants and their children probably included over several hundred people by World War I.[15]

Although these three groups of newcomers, the miners, the farmers around Harrah, and the smelter workers, formed the largest Polish communities in Oklahoma, other more independent Polish men and women also scattered across the state. In fact, by 1930, when the total number of Polish-born people and their children reached 3,888, they had spread out so evenly that thirteen counties had at least eighty Poles as permanent residents: Oklahoma and Lincoln, including a number of people from the Harrah area; Pittsburg and Okmulgee in the eastern coal-mining areas; and, Washington and Osage, including Bartlesville and surrounding settlements. Some Polish families moved into Tulsa County in the northeast, others into the northwestern wheat-producing counties of Major, Alfalfa, and Garfield, and still others into the southwestern cattle counties of Washita, Grady, and Comanche.[16] Only forty Polish families lived in Oklahoma City while another forty made their homes in the city of Tulsa. Most of the rest, some two-thirds of all of the Polish families in the state, lived in rural areas. Yet, neither in Tulsa County nor in any of these farming and ranching areas did a visible Polish settlement develop.[17]

These immigrant people were not wealthy and as housing figures from the depression year of 1930 indicate, many were hard pressed to meet their needs. Although seven Polish families in ten owned their own homes, the median value of these houses was only $1,854. Only fifteen out of 224 non-farm families owned homes worth as much as $1,000. Since Polish families tended to be larger than others, many of these modest dwellings were uncomfortably crowded.[18]

Over the next four decades, the state's Polish population declined in numbers and consolidated. Despite a post-World War II influx of refugees from Communist-controlled Poland, Oklahoma's Polish population (counting both first- and second-generation immigrants) stood at only 2,274 in 1970. By that time, 88 percent of these people lived in only seven counties: Oklahoma (867), Comanche (231), Garfield (95), and Cleveland, Washington, and Kay (each with 82). Polish residential patterns now clearly reflected those of the whole population, as Poles, along with other Oklahomans, gravitated towards the state's major urban centers. The metropolitan areas of Oklahoma

City, Tulsa, and Lawton, in particular, housed 827, 522, and 176 Polish people, respectively, at a time when only 471 others remained in rural locales. Enid and Norman probably had a number of Poles as well.[19]

These figures were somewhat misleading, however, since temporary residents probably inflated most of these county totals. Military personnel and their families may have accounted for many of the Poles listed in Oklahoma (Tinker A.F.B. in Midwest City), Comanche (Ft. Sill in Lawton), and Garfield (Vance A.F.B. in Enid) counties. Cleveland County's tally, on the other hand, included an unknown number of second-generation Polish students at the University of Oklahoma at Norman whose permanent homes were with their families in larger Polish communities in the Northeast and Midwest. Ponca City in Kay County, moreover, served until 1975 as headquarters for a province of Felician Nuns, many of whom were the daughters of Polish-born parents.[20]

The Sisters of St. Felix of Cantalicio of the Third Order of St. Francis trace their origins to the charitable work of noblewoman Sophia Truszkowska in the Russian-dominated Poland of the 1850s. Officially recognized by the Vatican in 1874, the Felician Sisters answered a call for help that same year when several of their number sailed for America to serve a community of Polish immigrants in Portage County, Wisconsin. As their numbers grew and their activities spread across the Midwest, the Felicians decided to move to an area of greater Polish concentration. In 1880, they established their American headquarters in Detroit, Michigan. From that point, Felician Sisters moved out over the country, coming to Ponca City in 1948.[21]

Ponca City first came to the attention of the Felicians the previous year when they learned that a group of Carmelite Fathers planned to sell the estate of E. W. Marland, oilman and tenth governor of Oklahoma. The Carmelites had purchased the Marland mansion in 1941 as a friary. In July 1948, the Felicians' Superior General, Mother Mary Simplicita Nehring, toured the grounds and immediately arranged to buy the property. Within a few months the first sisters moved into the renovated mansion.

Actually, the first Felicians had come to Oklahoma in 1946 at the urging of Bishop Eugene J. McGuinness and the Very Reverend Stephen A. Leven, then pastor of the Blackwell and Tonkawa parishes. Originally, eight sisters came from Lodi, New Jersey, to take charge of the Blackwell General Hospital. By the time that their order bought the Marland mansion and renamed it "Assumption

9

MAP 1

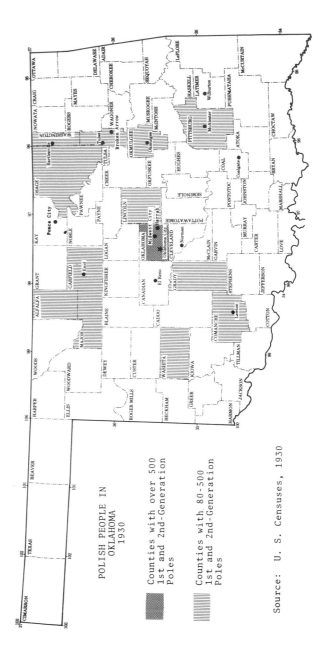

POLISH PEOPLE IN
OKLAHOMA
1930

Counties with over 500
1st and 2nd-Generation
Poles

Counties with 80-500
1st and 2nd-Generation
Poles

Source: U. S. Censuses, 1930

MAP 2

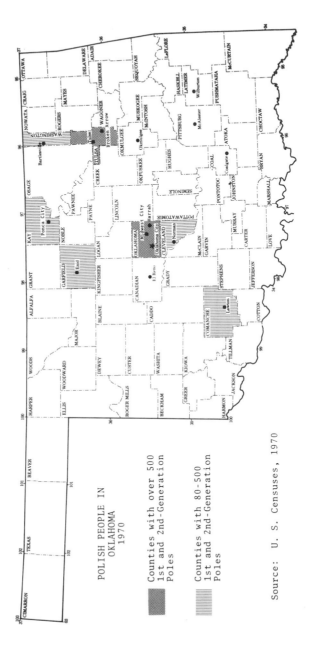

POLISH PEOPLE IN
OKLAHOMA
1970

Counties with over 500
1st and 2nd-Generation
Poles

Counties with 80-500
1st and 2nd-Generation
Poles

Source: U. S. Censuses, 1970

Villa," Felicians were staffing schools in Blackwell and Tonkawa, hospitals in Holdenville, Seminole, and Okarche, and a home for unwed mothers and their infants in Oklahoma City. Several provincial motherhouses sent women to work in these areas so the Felicians, who were by this time mostly second- and third-generation Polish-Americans, came to Oklahoma from a variety of northeastern locations.[22]

Although the Felicians planned to turn Assumption Villa into the motherhouse for a new western province, postwar developments suddenly elevated it to headquarters for the entire order. During the Second World War, Nazi officials had confiscated the Felician Generalate, the order's international motherhouse in Krakow, Poland. Resulting destruction, along with orders from the U.S. consulate for Americans to evacuate, caused many American-born sisters to return to the United States. Others who stayed, such as Mother Mary Simplicita remained in Poland, only to suffer confinement in German concentration camps. In 1946, as the order faced the prospect of rebuilding their motherhouse under Communist supervision, the war-weary Mother Simplicita became superior general of the organization. Although still planning a permanent home for the Felicians in Poland, she decided to move her provisional generalate to the more tranquil environs of Ponca City. Thus, in 1950, the old Marland mansion took on international significance for Polish Catholics as the headquarters of all the Felician Sisters.

Assumption Villa remained the provincial generalate until 1953 when Pope Pius XII asked the Felicians to transfer their operations to Rome. With Mother Simplicita's departure that year, the American sisters reverted to their previous plan and converted the Marland estate into the motherhouse of the Province of the Assumption of the Blessed Virgin Mary in Ponca City, Oklahoma. From that year until 1975, most Felician activities in the states west of the Mississippi centered there. Although based at the mansion (and appearing in the census figures of Kay County), these women worked in Texas, California, Missouri, Nebraska, Iowa, Kansas, and even in Alabama. In Oklahoma, Felicians continued to serve in the schools and hospitals as before, except in Seminole, but they also assumed control over three new schools, St. Philip Neri's in Midwest City, St. Mary's in Tulsa, and St. Anne's in Broken Arrow, as well as helping to staff Bishop McGuinness High School in Oklahoma City.

Uneasy in a once luxurious mansion located far from most of the people they served, the Felicians decided in 1975 to move their western headquarters into Franciscan territory at Rio Rancho, near Albuquerque, New Mexico. That year they sold the Marland property to the city, and by Christmastime, the last twenty-five sisters in residence departed for their new home, ending twenty-seven years of service to Oklahomans of all faiths from their Ponca City headquarters.[23]

The Felicians, however, were not the only members of religious orders to come to Oklahoma during the postwar years. The last and bravest of all Polish immigrants, in fact, were the refugee priests who came to the Sooner State in the late 1940s and early 1950s. Wartime contact with the Soviet "liberators" of their native Poland made many of these men reluctant to return to their homes after V-E Day. This group included a number of parish priests as well as others who belonged to specific orders, such as the Capuchin monks. Freed from German concentration camps or mustered out of the Polish armed forces in Western Europe, several of them accepted the invitation of Bishop McGuinness to make their permanent homes in Oklahoma.

Probably few people of Polish descent who live in Oklahoma today have ever seen Mount Radziminski, or ever heard of the civil engineer whose name it bears. Many Polish-Oklahomans are just beginning to rediscover their own heritage, now roughly four generations old. Probably only a few know of the Polish miners, farmers, smelter workers, and priests who carved out homes in the Sooner State, yet they deserve a place in the state's history. Their story is a tale of hard work and persistence against long odds that begins underground in the old Choctaw nation and ends for one Polish-Oklahoman with a place on the Oklahoma State Supreme Court.

Chapter 2

THE COAL MINERS OF THE McALESTER DISTRICT

Deep beneath the earth's surface in the lush green hills of the old Choctaw Nation, hundreds of Polish men, along with others from many nations, once risked death to extract Oklahoma's original money-making energy source. They mined soft bituminous coal, embedded under Indian lands that stretched eastward from the embryonic railroad community of McAlester. Beginning in 1873, hundreds of miners, whose numbers would one day reach into the thousands, climbed down into the underground shafts every year. In order to feed and clothe their families, they accepted work in some of the most dangerous mines in the United States.[1] Among those pick-and-shovel men were fellows such as John Zytkevich, Michael Nocek, and Louis Morovski—Polish immigrants whose experiences constituted a history of struggle both above and below ground.

Zytkevich, Nocek, Morovski, and hundreds of other Polish working men like them came to the coal mines of Indian Territory in hopes of finding a better future. Zytkevich and Nocek, in particular, saw little chance for economic advancement in the Poland of the 1880s and sailed for America, leaving their wives and children to join them later. Morovski made the same journey. All three gravitated to the Choctaw Nation where they took jobs in the McAlester coal-mining district.

At that point their paths diverged, illustrating the mixed fortunes of the men who entered the mines. Zytkevich, his name changed to "Daly" by a coal-company clerk who could not fit the original on a pay envelope, worked his way out of the mines. In time he became a grocer, a smalltime real estate agent, and a prosperous farmer, making his permanent home in Hartshorne, Oklahoma. Nocek, dubbed Nosock by a schoolteacher who approximated the name's English-language phonetic spelling, did not fare so well. In fact, he spent his entire working life under ground near Alderson where he died at age 64 in 1915, a victim of "miner's asthma" or black lung disease. Morovski proved even less fortunate. In the cold, clear words of an official government report from 1895: "March 12—Louis Morofski [sic] (Polander) miner, age 34 years; fatal." The report then explained: "This man mistook a [dynamite blast] which had been fired by another miner for his, and went back to the [firing area], when [his own] shot went off, killing him instantly, Hartshorne mine No. 1."[2]

These three men were not the first from their homeland to work in Oklahoma's coal mines. As early as 1876, Polish men had drifted into Indian Territory in search of work, only four years after operations had begun in the area.[3] During the half century of profitable excavations that followed, hundreds of Polish men and boys helped bring millions of dollars worth of the black fuel to the surface. As long as company whistles blew in the McAlester district, Polish people were on hand to load coal destined for the nation's furnaces.

Coal mines developed in the northern region of the Choctaw Nation primarily because of the efforts of a former Confederate soldier, J. J. McAlester, who arrived in Tobucksy, now McAlester, in 1870. McAlester had learned of extensive and little-known coal deposits east of that location. He and his partner, J. T. Hannaford, secured a trader's license from the Choctaw government and set up a general store in the Indian town.[4] Through marriage to a Chickasaw woman, McAlester gained joint citizenship in both the Chickasaw and Choctaw tribes. This civil status gave him the right to exclusive control over mining operations within one-mile radii of all mineral discoveries he might make. Together with several other intermarried whites McAlester then set up the Oklahoma Mining Company and began leasing his organization's subsurface rights to actual coal-producing companies, many of them owned by railroads. These latter groups immediately started stripmining operations. By 1899, twenty-two mines, both above and below ground, were in operation in the Indian nations. Nearly all of these were under railroad control.[5]

The railroad companies had to import labor for these mines. Local Indians were unwilling to enter the coal pits, much less the newly opened underground tunnels. The Choctaws and Chickasaws thought such work was degrading, and no amount of monetary

MAP 3

THE COAL MINING DISTRICTS
OF OKLAHOMA

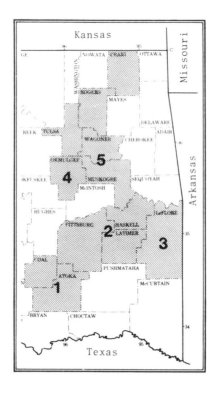

1   Coalgate

2   McAlester

3   Eastern

4   Henryetta

5   Northern

Source: Frederick Lynne Ryan, The Rehabilitation of Oklahoma
Coal Mining Communities (Norman, Okla., 1935), Map I, p. 14.

persuasion could change their minds. A number of black freedmen, once the slaves of Indian masters, were more willing to enter the mines since underground work brought a higher income than did subsistence farming. But there were too few of these men available, so producers quickly turned to the coal fields of the Midwest and the East. In the early 1870s, they sent agents into Pennsylvania to recruit white Americans and British immigrants to work in the McAlester District.

Within a few years the early American and British dominance in the work force disappeared. By 1908 only about a third of the miners in the former Choctaw Nation were the native-born sons of native-born fathers. Among the immigrants, the English, Scots, Welsh, and Irish gave way as early as 1890 to newcomers from a host of European countries. In 1874, the first Italians arrived, signalling the beginning of a large influx of working men, and later their families, from that country.[6] They were followed by a small number of Lithuanians and Russians (by 1875). A larger group of French and Belgian miners came to the Lehigh-Coalgate area by way of mines in Illinois (1881). A number of both Slovaks and Magyars came from the Austro-Hungarian Empire (1883). And groups of Mexicans (1890) and even Bulgarians (1908) came later. Some of these groups, especially the French and the Slovaks, became significant with the former once estimated at 900 people (1895) and the latter at 800 (1911). Several hundred Southern blacks, primarily from Alabama and West Virginia, also entered the labor force in the 1890s, most as strikebreakers.[7]

Among these international migrants were several hundred Polish people. Beginning in 1876, just three years after the mines opened, Polish laborers began to gather in the McAlester district. Each year a few more arrived until after 1896 when their numbers greatly expanded with the coming of the families and friends of the first men to migrate. The special statehood census of 1907 counted over fifty Polish-born people in McAlester, Krebs, Alderson, and Hartshorne, with many more scattered through the region.[8] By 1911, there were perhaps 800 first- and second-generation Poles in the Oklahoma coal fields.[9]

Few of these Polish people had experience as coal miners before coming to Indian Territory. A 1910 survey by the Dillingham Commission of some 175 Polish miners in Kansas and Oklahoma revealed that only a third had worked underground in the old country. Nearly half had tilled the soil.[10]

MAP 4

A.   The McAlester District
     (without Haskell County)

Dark-Shaded Area =   Light-Shaded Area =
Segregated Coal Lands Land Underlain by
of the Choctaw Nation bituminous coal or
(Source: Ryan, Coal   lignite (Source:
Mining Communities,   Hist. Atlas of Okla,
Map II, p. 42)   Map 71)

Sources: Frederick Lynne Ryan,
Coal Mining Communities (Norman
John W. Morris et al, Historica
Okla., 1976), Map 71; and, U.

Most of these people left Poland for the same general reasons as their emigrating countrymen, to better themselves economically, but the aggressive recruiting tactics of the mining companies and their agents brought them to the McAlester area. When the railroad men went into the eastern coal fields, they offered free, or at least deferred payment, transportation to the territory along with high wages upon arrival. Such promises convinced a good many miners, such as Bart Gornik, for example, to migrate.

Gornik, a Polish immigrant who had worked for Chicago's Armour Packing Company before getting work in the Pennsylvania mines, read the Oklahoma handbills. They seemed to promise steady work at $100 per month and that information was all he needed. Soon Gornik began collecting his pay in the McAlester District, earning money to bring his wife and children west. But he quickly discovered, as did the other miners, that the handbills greatly exag-

18

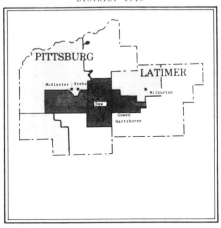

B. Townships with Polish-
    Born Residents in 1910

Dark-Shaded Area = Tps w/at least 20 Poles
Light-Shaded Area = Tps w/10 - 19 Poles

(Source: U. S. Census, 1910 (manuscripts)

e Rehabilitation of Oklahoma
)kla., 1935), Map II, p. 42;
tlas of Oklahoma, (Norman,
ensus, 1910 (manuscripts).

gerated the number of working days and thus overstated actual earnings.[11]

Such eastern miners could not supply enough manpower, so the agents looked for ways to get information to the immigrants before they arrived and settled. The company men began signing agreements with steamship lines, whereby the latter would encourage their steerage passengers to travel farther west. Until federal law banned the practice in 1890, agents also went to Europe and contracted with laborers there, agreeing to pay, or more likely to defer, the costs of their passages in exchange for commitments to enter the mines.

By the 1890s more and more new workers came to the McAlester area because they knew someone already there. Polish miner Andrew Waitrovich left his job in Bohemia just before World War I and came to Hartshorne because his brother-in-law there would help him find work.[12] Frank Posvkowski came straight from Poland to Alderson because there were "a lot of people there who had known him all his life."[13] In order to take advantage of such Old World ties, the coal companies financed transportation for miners' families and friends, with the costs deducted monthly from their employees' paychecks. By this arrangement, a miner such as John Zytkevich could bring his wife and three of their four children to Oklahoma. The fourth child, Stanley, could have come too if the company had sent more money. Although there were funds for four children's tickets, Stanley was old enough to require an adult fare so steamship authorities at Bremen, Germany, turned him away. Later, however, he did make the trip on his own.

Mrs. Zytkevich's journey was a heart-rending tale of the perils of immigration. Since they could not speak English, she and her family were unable to get food during the long train ride to Oklahoma. At one point she left the train, frightened though she was, in search of a concession stand. An angry porter immediately apprehended her and put her back on board. He thought she was trying to abandon the children. Thus, his well-intentioned efforts left the little ones with no supper.

Their desire for a large, contented, and heterogeneous labor force led coal companies to seek out workers from the eastern and southern European countries. Although the Americans and British were experienced miners who did their work well, they were not fond of frontier living conditions. Many longed for the advantages of more-settled mining communities that offered wider educational and employment opportunities for their children. Their familiarity with collective bargaining also caused some of them to organize and demand higher wages and safer working conditions.

Such demands were an anathema to the coal operators who sought to replace these men with less troublesome employees from the poorer, less democratic, and non-English speaking countries. Such people, they reasoned, would be more willing to accept the relative deprivations of frontier mining. One mine official, for example, wrote arrogantly of his black, Mexican, Austrian and Polish employees: "[They] do not aspire to the same standards of living that many classes of American workmen do . . . "[14] They also would be less likely to protest than would workers raised on the rhetoric of democracy and majority rule.

Language problems also would help keep these new employees in check. The bright lights of St. Louis, Oklahoma City, or even

McAlester would not tempt those who spoke no English. Companies also discovered that by recruiting from several different language groups, they could create their own Babels, retarding development of a labor union. Thus, non-English speaking workers such as the Poles personified stability and order to these employers.[15]

There was reason for concern over the quality of life for these workers. In the late nineteenth century, working conditions in the mines of the Choctaw Nation were not good for anyone, but were particularly bad for Poles. Management developed a preferential treatment system underground, and by 1911, a clear-cut pecking order emerged as the basis for promotions. At the top were white Americans and the Irish, Scots, English, and Welsh. Mine owners thought them the most troublesome as agitators, but also judged them most capable of handling responsibility. Below them were the Lithuanians, who had a reputation for remaining calm in emergencies. Next came the Magyars and northern Italians, followed by the southern Italians and Slovaks. Then there were the Poles, Russians, and American blacks, ranking above only the Mexicans in the estimation of many mine operators.[16] Few from these lower levels ever became "company men," the term for supervisors and other management officials.

The Poles, along with the members of several other groups, were victims of stereotyping that confined most of them to menial jobs. Few managers or owners respected the individual talents of their employees. Most probably agreed with that same company president when he wrote that "a great many men who work in the mines are incapable of doing any kind of labor . . . except by . . . physical force."[17] Less experienced in mining than most of the others when they came to this country, most Polish miners rather literally started at the bottom and stayed there.

Work as a common pick and shovel man was arduous at best. Six days a week during good times, the Polish miners and their fellow workmen rode down the main shaft to their assigned work levels. From there, they traveled on foot down the long entryways, indented about every thirty-five feet by the entrances to rooms where most of the digging took place. These rooms, roughly five feet high and ranging in diameter up to about fifty feet, resembled dark little fiefdoms. Pairs of working men controlled them. These two-man teams were invariably composed of people from the same nationality, and often from the same family, to guarantee harmony on the job. Their incomes depended on the quantity of high-grade coal that they loaded daily so each miner's compatibility with his "buddy" affected his own success. No wonder, as one retired miner put it, "The Polish guys all stuck together pretty much."[18]

Shoveling coal was hardly conducive to longevity. The main health problem was the foul air, saturated with coal dust and blasting powder, which permeated the underground tunnels. Unaware of the dangers of black lung disease, the miners used to joke about their congested working conditions.[19] Accidents were all too possible, and no laughing matter. Between March 1885 and April 1906, 187 miners lost their lives in *major* disasters in the mines fields of Indian Territory, all but twenty dying in explosions. About another 200 perished during the same period in "minor" mishaps involving fewer than five fatalities in each. One accident alone, a horrendous explosion at Krebs Mine No. 11 on January 7, 1892, trapped nearly 300 men below ground. At least sixty-eight men were lost and double that figure were burned or maimed.[20]

From management's viewpoint, all such accidents from the most trivial fall to the monstrous explosion at Krebs were the fault of the miners. The accident problem in Oklahoma was critical, they admitted, but company negligence had nothing to do with it. People caused accidents, ignorant and careless people who should never have been in the mines in the first place. The companies that had deliberately introduced non-English speaking people into mining, now claimed that such workers endangered themselves by their inability to read and understand warning signs. Voicing the company position, the Dillingham Commission of 1911 concluded that: " . . . the ignorance of the foreigner as to the English language brings not only great danger to himself, but to every man working in the mine with him."[21]

Until 1894, Oklahoma miners earned about five cents a ton for the coal they brought to the surface, or about twenty cents per day more than men in the Pennsylvania fields. Thereafter, unionization, changing economic conditions, and attempted wage cuts lessened the regional advantage that Oklahoma miners had enjoyed, keeping pay levels volatile until the depression of the 1930s.[22]

Miners in the new lands did not earn princely incomes, however. Employers paid them on the basis of the number of tons they produced each day, and the amount of money in the miners' weekly pay envelopes depended on the number of days the mines operated. Operations, in turn, depended on the fluctuating fuel demands of American industry. It was weakest during depression years, such as

Richard M. Bernard

in the mid-nineties, and in 1907–1908, and strongest during wartime, especially 1914–18.

If few of the miners understood the industrial laws of supply and demand, all knew that getting work in the mines was a day-to-day proposition. Each evening, the miners learned by means of the company whistles whether to report the next morning. Like prisoners about to hear the ruling of the court, families waited each night for the sound that told whether their men could work the next day.[23]

The average number of working days per year in Indian Territory rarely exceeded 160. Even after statehood when the number of work days increased, miners could expect bad years such as 1908 when they averaged only 175 days in the mines. Such limited work opportunities greatly distorted weekly pay figures. For example, according to the State Department of Labor, the apparently substantial weekly wage rates of 1908–1909 disguised a relatively low level of real annual earnings: " . . . when you stop to consider that the miners are employed [only] five to eight months in a year, they are not making much more than the average street laborer at $1.75 per day."[24]

Working under such on-again, off-again conditions, Polish miners fared about the same as most. In 1910, despite earning daily wages which, at $2.48, averaged 14 cents below the figure for all miners, the Poles probably brought home as much or more during the year as did their fellow workers. Because they worked more days each year, they earned a little more than the average annual salary for all miners of $448.[25]

Polish miners, along with those of other nationalities, generally maintained rather meager standards of living, which their modest housing accommodations demonstrated. Throughout the coal districts, miners lived in substandard dwellings, especially individuals who rented company-owned homes. Usually these sprang up around newly-opened mine shafts where no other housing existed. Regardless of their location, they left much to be desired since the companies spent as little as possible on construction.

Naturally, with cost the only serious consideration, these houses were humble at best. As John Zytkevich's daughter remembered: "They were not huge homes because the Rock Island Coal Company built [them] and about all they'd have maybe was one bedroom or two bedrooms and maybe a kitchen. . . . "[26] The typical company house was a one-story frame structure with three to five rooms, each from twelve to fourteen feet on a side. Normally, all houses in a given community followed the same floor plan. If they were painted at all

23

they bore a standard, dull red barnlike color. Workmanship was terrible, and there were no indoor plumbing facilities. Water came from centrally located community wells.[27]

These dwellings, which rented monthly for about $1.80 to $2.00 per room, became the homes of not only individual mining families but also various single men for whom no hotels or barracks were available. Families took in such men, generally from their own nationality groups, to help pay their own rent. Very few of the miners' wives worked outside their own homes; only four, none of them Polish, out of 418 Kansas and Oklahoma wives surveyed in 1910 did so. The main means for a family to supplement the father's wages was by renting beds to young men.

As a rule, the families assumed little responsibility for their guests. Usually they provided them with a daily cup of either coffee or soup and with access to the cookstove so that they could fix their own meals. The men could have their dinners prepared for an additional charge. Under these or similar terms, in 1910 about one mining family in five took in renters, though that figure may have been higher for Polish families. Overall boarders and lodgers probably boosted family income by only about 10 percent.[28]

The general upkeep of these homes, and of others that private individuals later built near the mines, depended on the proportion of the houses sold to their occupants. Rarely did renters maintain their homes as well as did property owners, though a lack of cash minimized everyone's hopes for home improvements.

Immigrant miners felt as strongly about their homes as did native Americans, and worked hard to purchase and maintain them. Home ownership was a matter of pride for them. Polish people, in particular, came to America with the firm goal of regaining a piece of the earth, however small it might be. For many, the major objective was "to own a home and to get a piece of land, and work the land and make the garden . . . so they could have a cow and some chickens and anything for their family."[29] No wonder they kept purchased homes in much better condition than neighboring rent houses.

Whether the miners owned or rented their homes, they chose them primarily on the basis of their locations. When it came to housing, even in the smallest communities, members of the same nationalities tended to cluster together. Only one immigrant group, the Italians of Krebs, became large enough to dominate an entire mining town. Other groups, including the Poles, did establish pluralities in various sections of almost every community.[30]

Most of the little mining settlements in the McAlester district had well-defined Polish sections. These were not exclusively Polish, but carried clear reputations as Polish turf. Julian Shamasko, a retired Polish miner from McAlester, remembered a "Polish Town" in Gowen and a "little place in the road" called Frog Town which was "all Polish."[31] In Alderson, there was a tripartite division of territory. "Polish people and Lithuanian people lived [together]. And then in another part of town, Italian people. And then in another part . . . Americans."[32] In fact, contemporaries considered all land between the railroad tracks and the highway as Polish. "They were all Polish," claimed Mrs. Shamasko. "Every one of the houses, there was not an English person there."[33] Hartshorne, the largest of these little towns, had a neighborhood known as "Polish Street." Not one street at all, this area, just across the railroad tracks from the business district, stretched four or five blocks in each direction. Within its bounds lived nearly all of the Polish coal miners in the city.

Within these little communities two generations of Polish children grew to maturity, married, and started families. In the early days most of these children learned to speak Polish first, but gradually they, and especially their younger brothers and sisters, learned English from their non-Polish playmates.

Polish girls typically stayed home with their mothers and learned housekeeping and cooking skills. On occasion they might accept temporary employment picking and chopping cotton, but such instances of outside work were rare. The boys, on the other hand, usually followed their fathers into the mines. Unable to start work legally until age sixteen, many Polish boys left school early anyway. By one means or another, including falsifying their birth dates, they soon entered the tunnels. Few families could afford the luxury of idle sons in school so it was quite unusual for a Polish boy to stay in school beyond the eighth grade.[34] Mrs. Clementina Gornik claimed, for example, that her husband "went to work when he was eleven. They were allowed to take [such youngsters] inside the coal mines," she recalled, "because they were working beside the fathers."[35]

By the time that the boys reached their late twenties and the girls their late teens they were ready to marry. Since most of the young men spoke only Polish, they naturally selected marriage partners from their own group. At least until World War I, their brides were uniformly Polish and Catholic. As one woman put it, "they married their own kind, and they married their own religion — it's not like mixing now, you know."[36]

Polish weddings, which were at least all-day affairs, offered everyone in the local parish an opportunity for fellowship and entertainment. This pleasure came at a price, however, for all who attended had to "break the plate" to help endow the young couple with a dowry. The bride's or groom's parents bought plain white dinner plates, and while everyone danced, they set them out on the floor. Each guest had to toss silver dollars at a plate, trying to break it, and by custom, each had to keep trying, always using a new coin, until he succeeded. Some brides and grooms thus began their married lives with several hundred dollars in silver.

Polish families, like those of other Catholic immigrant groups, were large, and would have been even larger if the parents had married at younger ages. In the coal-mining communities, as elsewhere in America, therefore, family activities dominated Polish social life.

Growing and preparing food, for example, were family-centered activities. According to one Polish ex-miner, "every foreigner" had a garden. They grew corn, sweet potatoes and other vegetables, then stored them for the winter in tin cans ordered from Sears and Roebuck. Several families raised pigs and some had other animals as well. Many mothers taught their daughters to prepare dishes from the old country—*pierogis* (a noodle dish like Italian ravioli), *kielbasa* (sausage) and many others for the big evening meals during the week and the noon meal on Sunday.

Most family recreation centered on front porches and front rooms where Polish people came together to sit and visit. Frequently, "they would come home from work and, after supper, they'd gather up in somebody's home—get on a porch—a whole bunch of them and they'd . . . talk and laugh and enjoy theirselves."[37] Often times, after the evening whistles had blown, someone would bring out a fiddle or a guitar, and everyone would sing. On Saturday nights, the Polish families would all converge at one home or another to dance, talk, and drink "Choctaw beer," brewed especially for the occasion by some of the miners. Although it was sometimes possible to escape this family-oriented environment, few chose to do so. Some might go to the opera house at Hartshorne or Krebs, others might try the honky-tonks of the latter town. In later years, some might even ride into McAlester for a picture show. But such disloyalty was rare, for most confined their social lives to their own groups.

Tenaciously loyal to Catholicism, these Polish miners strongly supported the several churches of the area. Often built by Benedictines based at Sacred Heart Mission, near Konawa, these congregations were as strong as any of the Roman faith in the Twin Territories. Poles were especially visible among parishioners at Hartshorne and Gowen although in neither place did they form a majority. When Polish children did attend school, it was usually in parochial academies.[38]

Despite this picture of community spirit and contentment, a great many miners, including a number of Poles, found life and work in the Oklahoma mines unsatisfactory. During the first twenty years of operations in Indian Territory, these men worked ten- to twelve-hour days under very dangerous conditions. Yet because of temporary shutdowns, they sometimes brought home as little as $30 per month. They earned nothing for the time spent clearing "brushings," loose rock and soil around the veins, and nothing for the unavoidable slack coal, chunks small enough to pass through a four-inch screen and thus, from the company's viewpoint, not marketable. Of course, there were no such things as retirement benefits and workmen's compensation.

Pay envelopes, already docked for slack coal production, shrank further with deduction for the residential permits necessary for all whites living on Choctaw land, school taxes, house or room rents, and doctors' fees. This last, about one dollar per month, was especially upsetting to the men. Few of them had faith in the company doctors, since these medical men were reluctant to diagnose "miner's asthma" as a work-induced disability.[39]

Even with wages in hand, few miners were free from the pervasive control of their employers. They still had to buy at the company-owned stores. In early times, mine employees patronized these high priced retail outlets largely because they had little choice. Throughout the first twenty-five years of mining in the area, most coal companies paid their personnel in scrip, redeemable only at the company stores. Besides, even when workers did receive cash, they faced the prospects of long walks to towns like Wilburton and Hartshorne if they wanted to trade at independently owned establishments.

After the turn of the century, when miners took home their pay in real money and when more stores were accessible, many families continued to shop at company stores. They were conveniently located in mining camps and offered credit to their customers. If a miner needed goods between paydays, he could still draw scrip as advances against his wages. As in older times, the miners had to spend this money at company-owned or franchised stores.[40]

Living and working under such conditions, the miners as a group proved highly receptive to overtures from union organizers who began appearing in the McAlester district in the early 1880s. By 1884, the Knights of Labor had enlisted fifteen hundred members. A decade later, their organization won a major strike, thereby minimizing the impact of a depression-era wage cut. The United Mine Workers succeeded the Knights in 1898, and in 1903, successfully concluded a territory-wide, three-and-a-half-year strike for recognition and an eight-hour day at an average pay scale of $2.56. This agreement became the fundamental basis for all subsequent negotiations, and remained in force until after World War I. Another massive strike and settlement in 1919, and an accompanying agreement in 1924 brought daily wages up to $7.50, though inflation consumed much of the miners' apparent gain. Later that same year, the coal companies reneged on the contract provoking yet another strike. This time, however, the operators won, breaking the union for all practical purposes, and by 1927, wages were back to $5.00.[41]

Throughout these labor-management disputes, Polish workers stayed with their union. They never assumed leadership positions, but stood firm with the rank and file. There was no record of any Pole ever working as a strikebreaker.

Although the American economy as a whole expanded at an incredible pace during the Roaring Twenties, the Oklahoma coal-mining industry followed the state's agriculture into steady decline. Small firms felt the crunch of competition first, as larger operations cut their prices to meet the challenge of petroleum. The big companies then suffered in turn as the nation and the state shifted to oil. One by one, they cut back their operations by closing less efficient mine shafts. By 1932 the Rock Island Coal Company of Hartshorne still employed over 1,000 men, but no other firm maintained a payroll of more than 180. Within a few more years the Rock Island mines also shut down.[42]

First hundreds then thousands of miners lost their jobs during these years and most of them, including perhaps three-quarters of the Poles, left the coal-mining areas permanently. Some found jobs driving trucks and operating machinery in Oklahoma City, Tulsa, and Muskogee. Others joined the waves of Oklahomans who migrated to southern California to work in the fruit and vegetable harvests.

Most of the Poles, however, moved to the industrial centers of the upper Midwest. According to several Polish people who still live in the McAlester district, most went to Chicago and Detroit where there were already large Polish communities. There they found jobs in the meat-packing and automobile industries. Others went to work for city governments as maintenance men. Julian Shamasko got on at International Harvester in Chicago. Andrew Waitrovich, Jr., found a place at Kimberly-Clark's paper mill in Niagara, Wisconsin.

Usually such departures began with letters to relatives and friends in the northern cities asking about jobs, churches, and living accommodations. Often replies came with words of assurance. The families next sent their most employable members, often the oldest sons but sometimes fathers or daughters, to find work and to observe conditions firsthand. "Then, pretty soon now, the boy would get a job and he'd work and he'd send money back home to his parents, and the next thing you know, the parents would pick up and leave."[43] Occasionally, the parents decided to stay where they were, but rarely did a child return. By the mid-1930s only a handful of the oldtimers remained.

These people left behind a legacy of hard work and cooperative action to improve their fortunes in life. Although they rarely gained leadership positions at either the work place or the union hall, they always shouldered their fair share of the burdens. They were relatively content with the pleasures of family and community, and their prospects rose and fell with the strength of their own arms, with the muscle of the United Mine Workers, and with the price of the coal they shoveled. Theirs was an honorable story of toil under some of the most adverse working conditions in industrial America.

Chapter 3

THE FARMERS OF HARRAH

About twenty miles east of Oklahoma City, where U.S. Highways 62 and 270 intersect near the banks of the North Canadian River, stands the city of Harrah. All around it is the oldest and most thoroughly Polish community in Oklahoma. In fact, several of the Polish farms to the southeast predate the founding of the city itself. Originally settled by farmers transplanted from central Arkansas, Harrah, and St. Teresa's Parish, have served four generations of Polish-Oklahomans as the mother community in the Sooner State.

The ten original Polish families to settle there in the spring of 1892 saw a gently rolling landscape that stretched far beyond their view, northward to Kansas, southward to the Red River, and as far west as the Gypsum Hills. Called the Red Bed Plains by geographers, these lands offered the settlers little to excite the eye or obstruct human vision. What passed for hills in this new territory were only subtle stirrings of the earth's surface that had caused slight rises, places where the land now peaked above the cottonwood, redbud, and scrub oak trees. Only the meandering North Canadian River disrupted the harmony of these plains. In its centuries-old wanderings, the river had excavated rich bottom lands north of its bed. Along its south bank it had carved out abrupt, twenty-foot bluffs, indented by small canyons and gulches.

In late spring, however, the muddy red-clay soil of the region revealed a feature that would curse the early working days of the new settlers. It was grass, not modern day Bermuda, Johnson, or crab grass, but natural, "blue stem" prairie grass, tough and deep rooted. At a minimum it grew above a farmer's waist and quite often rose above the eye level of his wife. Although picturesque to the artistic eye, this grass meant long, hard work for agriculturalists who had to clear fields.[1]

As they initially gazed on the land, these Polish people were probably unaware of the devil that lurked beneath the earth's surface. The family heads who had filed homestead claims the previous September, came too late to see the grass at its most vibrant stage. By that time, the August sun had scorched the land, drying out the soil and baking its vegetation to a golden brown. Although these men must have pulled up clumps of the dead grass and examined its lengthy root systems, they could hardly have foreseen the back-breaking labor necessary to remove and replace this growth.

The newcomers did not see grass, however, but home and and opportunity. The very flatness of the red earth made possible the vast expanse of blue sky, equally familiar to the American cowboy and the Polish farmer. In fact, the breadth of the Polish plain was the chief characteristic of these people's motherland and the one which made it so vulnerable to foreign invasion. As they looked across the rolling terrain, the native Poles may well have felt at home. Such is the feeling which comes to a true plainsman as he views the distant horizons that leave more than enough room for unchecked movement. As a bonus, the settlers could have turned westward and enjoyed brilliant sunsets of red and gold, an ample compensation for the dusty air that made such beauty possible.

The land represented opportunity. Regardless of its natural limitations, this land seemed the best on earth to them because it was available. It was available, not just to the wealthy as in conquered Poland, but open, or so it seemed, to everyone on a "first-come" basis. Free land available to poor people! This had been unthinkable in far-off Europe—unthinkable even in nearby Arkansas! Ownership and opportunity: this was what the first Polish farmers really envisioned as they surveyed their new property.

This new land came under Polish ownership through a complex series of governmental actions centering in Washington. Originally under nominal Spanish and French control, the Harrah area, indeed the entirety of Oklahoma save the Panhandle, came into American hands as a part of the Louisiana Purchase of 1803. Primarily under Presidents Andrew Jackson and Martin Van Buren, the territory west of Arkansas became a dumping ground for Indians from the south-eastern states. The area around Harrah, in particular, fell under the joint authority of the Creek and Seminole nations. In 1856 a new U.S.–Seminole treaty divided the communal lands, and in the process, split in two the future environs of the city of Harrah. The area north of the North Canadian went to the Creeks while everything south, including the heart of the future community, became Seminole property.

This division proved only temporary. In 1872, Congress sliced off a piece of Seminole land, west of where most tribesmen lived, and placed it under the joint control of a band of Shawnees and a newly-arrived group of Pottawatomies from Kansas. This property contained the southeast corner of modern Oklahoma County, including Elk and Pottawatomie townships and the city of Harrah. Eleven years later, the government gave Creek land just above that of the Shawnees and Pottawatomies to a clan of Kickapoos.

In July 1890 the Pottawatomies and Shawnees agreed to cede their undeveloped western real estate back to the government and, under the terms of the Dawes Act, as amended, to accept individual land allotments. These negotiations cleared the way for a second Oklahoma land run, just to the east of the Unassigned Lands already grabbed up by the '89ers. Thus, on September 22, 1891, this ground became the possession of the most athletic of thousands of white men lined up on its border. Later settlers then repeated the whole process on May 23, 1895, opening the Kickapoo territory in the fifth land run. Thus it was by speed of foot that Polish people became landowners in Oklahoma County.[2]

Harrah's original Polish homesteaders came to the region by way of the Polish farming community of Marche, Arkansas. Located in Pulaski County, some sixteen miles northwest of Little Rock, Marche had drawn its first Polish settlers in 1877. Within three years a number of additional Polish families had also arrived. Polish by birth and German by nationality, most of these people, along with their American-born children, had come indirectly to Arkansas from points in the northern United States. While many of them had worked in American industries, they all sought farms on the new land.[3] In Marche they bought property from railroad companies for between three and six dollars per acre. Many of the earliest paid cash while others took up to three years to complete their purchases and redeem their mortgage notes. Still others became tenant farmers.

Unfortunately, there was good reason for these low land prices. The ground was sandy and rocky, guaranteeing poor crop yields. Many became discouraged, and among these, a number looked westward to the Indian lands. By the early fall of 1891, many were ready to make a move.

Theirs was a communal migration. The question of exactly which family arrived first in those early days of spring made little difference either to contemporaries or to their descendants. The oldest account says simply that "ten Polish families . . . came here in covered wagons from the state of Arkansas in the year 1892." By the end of that year, these included:

Mr. and Mrs. Joseph Blochowiak (five children)
Mr. and Mrs. Lawrence Drzewiecke (six children)
Mr. and Mrs. Michael Dreiviecki (five children)
Mr. and Mrs. John Jezewski (two children)
Mr. and Mrs. Ike Jezewski (five children)
Mr. and Mrs. Valentine Makoske (two children)
Mr. and Mrs. Adolph Miller (three children)
Mr. Andrew Nowakowski (mother, two brothers, three sisters)
Mr. and Mrs. George Olejniczak (two children)
Mr. and Mrs. Martin Wozniak (nine children).[4]

Generally, the men in these households came first, gaining legal claim to the lands in the fall and then returning for their families in the winter. There were two exceptions to this pattern. John Jezewski did not make the initial trip. Instead, he bought the claim of another man and with his family, followed behind the main party by about a month. Andrew Nowakowski, nominal head of his family at age twenty-one, learned of the Oklahoma situation via a letter from the early pioneers. He came alone, later in 1892. After working about a year he sent for his widowed mother, brothers and sisters.

The community's founding fathers were rather mature adults with their families almost complete. Lawrence Drzewiecke was 55, two years older than George Olejniczak. Except for Andrew Nowakowski, the others were probably in their late thirties or early forties. Most had been in the United States for a number of years, and several may have sailed from Germany together in 1872. All but Nowakowski had been married for a number of years. As a group, they had children still living with them who ranged in age from about one month to 16 years. Two men, Ike Jezewski and George Olejniczak, had remarried after the deaths of their first wives.

Victoria Olejniczak Jezewski, George's daughter, had died in Marche in the summer of 1891, leaving her husband Ike and five children under the age of eleven. In such cases, Polish traditions strongly urged remarriage. Given that fact and faced with the prospect of taming a frontier with one hand while caring for youngsters with the other, Ike married again within six months of Victoria's death. His new bride was Katy Rominski, nearly twenty years his junior and "fresh off the boat" from Poland. She had traveled as a companion and helper to another woman who with her two children was going to join her husband in this country. Soon after their arrival, Katy and Ike wed and, along with Ike's children, they headed west. They joined, among others, Ike's former father-in-law, his second wife Barbara and her two young ones.

As they daily followed the winter sun across the sky, the cold northerly winds swept the plains and whipped the canvas tops of their wagons. The February rains added more discomfort by muddying the trails ahead and turning river crossings into real hazards. At least two families found the going particularly slow because they brought heavy iron stoves with them. At the end of their journey, each family found a homestead of 160 acres. The government required little in return for this land. The newcomers had paid their filing fees and would soon pay their taxes, not with money, but with labor. Household heads could satisfy the tax collector simply by working on the public roads several days each year. The only other thing the government asked was persistence. Each family had to remain on their claims and improve them over five years time to gain clear title to their properties.

Such official generosity could hardly have come to a more needy and deserving people. "My dad was awful poor," recalled Andrew Jorski, one of Ike Jezewski's sons. "He had a tough time here! Nothing to eat."[5] Indeed the whole community found the going rough in the early days. Housing was substandard to say the least. "Since this was wilderness," wrote chronicler Joseph Janowiak many years later, "these people lived in their covered wagons. Some made dugouts in the ground until they were able to build their little homes."[6] Ike's daughter, Mary Nowakowski, recalled that her family lived underground for a year until her Grandfather Olejniczak found enough time to prepare new lodgings for them. He used the canvas from the wagon and made a tent. There they stayed for another two years before moving into a one-room cabin, roughly ten feet on each side. Although this new abode proved clearly advantageous when the winds shifted to the northwest, the family did not soon forget their first home. As if to remind them of the early days, the cabin still had a dirt floor.[7]

Housing, however, was of only secondary importance. On the Oklahoma frontier, the first order of business was food, and the effort spent procuring it left little time for other activities. Unfortunately, the grasses, along with the lengthy roots of the scrub oaks, were too stubborn for immediate removal. Adding to these natural problems, a shortage of plows meant long delays before agricultural production could begin. In fact, simply clearing enough land to support a family often took several years.

In the meantime, people had to eat. Admittedly, their diets were hardly above the minimum necessary for hard work on the frontier, but they still required expenditures. Mary Nowakowski remembered that "We live[d] on pancakes, a little coffee, a little sowbelly."[8] To these staples, the pioneers added wild fruits, grapes, plums, blackberries, mulberries, crab apples, hickory nuts, walnuts, and persimmons. Boiled rabbit was also a frequent dish. But since staples did not grow on trees, family treasuries quickly dwindled. Purchased bags of flour became rare treats causing simultaneous joy for the children and financial anxiety for the parents.

Soon the men left the farms in the care of the women and children and searched for outside employment. In the early days, however, few jobs were available, and thus they were lucky to find work on the railroad. The Atchison, Topeka, and Santa Fe, then in process of extending tracks from Kansas to the Gulf of Mexico, hired several of the men.

These jobs came at emotional costs. They required weekly separations from wives and children. Each Monday morning the men set out for the ever-more-distant construction sites. They would not see their families again until the following Saturday. When they did return, they usually carried with them a week's supply of groceries from the general store located about ten miles from most of the farms.

The construction foremen, moreover, forced the men to change their names. Blochowiak became simply "Block" while Drzewiecke shortened to "Drew." Since there was no handy English name like Jezewski, the bosses just chopped it back to "Jorski" with a hard Anglican j-sound replacing the rolling y-sound of the original name pronounced "yo-rev-sky."[9]

While many of the men worked on the railroad, others helped the women and children clear the fields. Community spirit was high and most cooperated in this effort. Andrew Nowakowski, for example, obtained a plow and with it, prepared Ike Jorski's fields for planting. "My husband—we weren't married yet," recalled Mary Nowakowski,

"he had four steers and we had two and we put to the plow six steers.
. . . You could hear the hooves: 'clack, clack, clack!'"[10] In three or
four years time, most farms yielded sufficient harvests for the men
to return to the land.

Although each family planted a garden and grew food for its
own table, the main agricultural enterprise that involved whole households was the production of cash crops. For many years, the little
community's net income depended on the prices for cotton and corn
in such faraway places as New Orleans and Chicago. Later, alfalfa
and wheat surpassed these products in importance. In the meantime,
whole families worked together to plow, cultivate, and harvest the
crops, for even very small hands could pick the bolls of cotton.

At the end of a hard day's work, farmers looked forward to the
simple pleasures of home. These included homemade bread and
such Polish delicacies as *kielbasa* (sausage), *kluski* (noodles), *maciek*
(a dish made from lamb's liver) and *czarnina* (duck-blood soup
seasoned with prunes, raisins, and vinegar). On Saturday nights, the
whole Polish community gathered for singing, dancing, and chatting
about the week's events. George Olejniczak would bring his accordion

The Frank Lutomski family picking cotton near Harrah, Oklahoma, ca. 1895. Courtesy
of Mr. John L. Hopcus.

and others, their fiddles and bass guitars. Over the years, the songs would lean heavily to that branch of country and western music now called "western swing." But in the early days, the polkas, waltzes, and schottisches of old Europe prevailed. On rare occasions the alcoholic spirits of the evening took over and fights erupted. This was hardly the rule, however, as Hattie Jorski, John's eighty-three-year-old daughter-in-law recalled. "They got along even if they got drunk. They'd just lay down and sleep, and get up and start jumping again." Was it moonshine they drank? "Oh no, they had the beer and whiskey and stuff like that. . . . It was a good old time."[11]

One of the best musicians joined the community several years after its founding. Polish-born fiddler Anthony Wilkowski arrived from Minnesota in the mid-1890s, bringing his parents, wife, and four of their children. Other Poles also arrived before the turn of the twentieth century, most of them having stopped in other American states along the way. The Zawiszas and the Cynars came from Nebraska; the Walterses from Illinois, by way of Colorado; the Gorneys from Marche, Arkansas. As in the case of their predecessors, all of these people became farmers.

Among them was Apolinary Magott and his wife, the former Mary Chwalinski from St. Louis. Magott, who had left Poland as an eighteen-year-old youth, initially migrated to Marche where he joined his brother, a Catholic priest. In Poland, he had worked as a lowly herdsman, shepherding a flock of 200 geese, but in Arkansas, he earned enough money to buy a farm of his own. Yet despite such success, he and Mary decided to join friends in the new land. Accordingly, Magott sold his farm for "400 gold pieces"—so heavy that they "almost pulled the pockets out of his pants." Together with the Kusek family and two single men, Thomas and Martin Kaezka, he drove his wagon westward. Mary, who had recently lost a baby, could not travel so she and three-year-old Frank came later by train.[12]

In-migration continued in the early 1900s and included the first family to arrive directly from Poland. Barbara Olejniczak's son, Anthony Hensel, his wife, and their five children came at her urging. Unfortunately, the Olejniczaks had no room for their penniless kin, and so they had to find other lodgings. For over six months the new immigrants lived with Andrew and Mary Nowakowski until they could rent a farm of their own.

Others also used the Nowakowski cabin as a port of arrival, in part because of Andrew's promotional efforts. Hoping to populate

37

the region with Polish people, he placed a notice in a widely circulated Polish-language newspaper, Chicago's *Kuryer Polske.* In it, he claimed that wonderful opportunities awaited the newcomer to the territory. This effort proved too successful for personal privacy. In Mary Nowakowski's words the notice boasted that "here in Oklahoma is healthy and everything is real nice, and those people in Texas got that paper and they read that paper, and everybody came to [our house]. They know our name."[13]

The *Kuryer* did indeed reach Texas, and in particular, the Polish farming community at Bremond in Robertson County. Some, like Joseph Klimkowski, had already left there for Harrah. Klimkowski, a native of Huta-Drohobichka in Austrian Poland, may have moved his family to Oklahoma as early as 1895.[14] The Nowakowski notice, however, probably triggered the more substantial migration of some twenty families in about 1906.[15]

Although most of the original settlers had roots in Prussian Poland, the great majority of the newcomers came from Galicia, the Austrian area. As a result, in 1910 Elk and Dewey townships, where most of the people from Bremond settled, had mostly Austrian Poles. In fact, of 129 first-generation Polish immigrants, a full 108 had served the Hapsburg emperor. By contrast Pottawatomie township, south of Harrah where most of the Marche group lived, was home for 30 Polish-born people, 10 of whom had been subjects of the German Kaiser.[16]

Despite diverse political backgrounds, these individuals, like the vast majority of Polish people everywhere, were united in their Catholic faith. From their first days in Oklahoma, they formed more of a parish than a conventional American community. They lacked only a priest and the official sanction of the Church hierarchy.

In the early years, the people met in one another's homes on Sundays and on holy days of obligation to say the rosary and sing hymns. By 1893, various itinerant priests, the first a Father Sculiak, began arriving by horseback or by buggy, once or twice a month. These men said mass over kitchen tables, expropriated for use as altars. Later, as the little congregation grew, these services shifted to the White Turkey Schoolhouse on the Adolph Miller farm, three miles south of the emerging city.

Church and town soon developed almost simultaneously. In 1897, the Catholic group, overwhelmingly Polish, obtained a parcel of land from one of its non-Polish members, John Beal. Quickly, a building committee of Beal, John Block, and Mike Drew organized

MAP 5

Eastern
Oklahoma County
and the
Harrah Area
1978

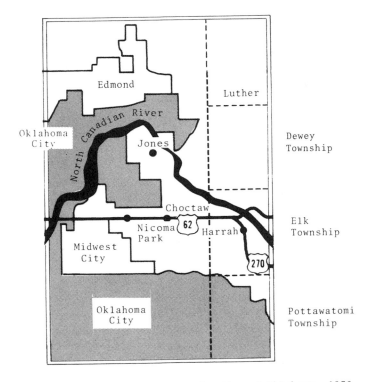

Sources: Official State Transportation Map of Oklahoma, 1978, and U. S. Census.

and began soliciting funds. Within a year's time, the Church of St. Teresa of Avila took on a physical form. In 1898 volunteer workers nailed the last oak plank in place. Originally built on the present location of the parish cemetery, the building was moved uphill to its present site and expanded some nine years later.

Earlier, in 1891, tiny post offices called Cavet and Pennington had popped up on either side of the North Canadian. Construction of a new railroad, the Choctaw, Oklahoma, and Gulf, in 1896, however, prompted consolidation of these facilities at a new station house, just south of the river itself, at a place where Irishman E. W. Sweeney operated a ferry service. Sweeney, who later married Martin Wozniak's daughter Rosa, became postmaster and gave his name to the location. In 1898, however, "Sweeney" became the town of Harrah, when merchant Frank Harrah bought and platted most of the surrounding countryside.[17]

The year 1898 also brought the first Polish wedding in the area, the indirect result of a wagon ride to market. With her son's future in mind, Mary Nowakowski, Andrew's mother, asked to join Andrew and neighbor Ike Jorski as they delivered a load of cotton to McCloud. En route, Mary abruptly exercised her parental prerogative and popped the question. "Jorski," she asked, "you don't care if my son Andrew married your Mary?" Though probably startled at first, Ike Jorski went home laughing and announced the match to his shocked and tearful fifteen-year-old daughter. From Ike's point of view, the facts were clear. Nowakowski, a good churchman, owned a three-bedroom house and had only his mother to look after it. That was all Ike Jorski needed to know, and, as in most Polish households, the father's word was law. The wedding took place about six weeks later with the bride crying right up to the start of the ceremony.[18]

The parish passed another important milestone a decade later when its first full-time priest took up residence in the newly con-structed rectory. In 1908, Father Stanislaus Lepich began ministering to the flock of some forty to fifty families, a group large enough to found a Rosary Altar Society for women within five years after the priest's arrival. Such numbers, however, also proved large enough for internal conflicts to arise.[19]

The tenures of Fathers Anthony Suwalski (1909–20) and Adam Oraczewski (1920–21) were turbulent eras in the parish's history. During the time of the former, the problems were both religious and political in nature, as they centered on a subgroup among the Bremond immigrants. Included among the Texan newcomers were a

MARYJO

KRÓLOWO

POLSKI

JESTEM PRZY
TOBIE,

PAMIĘTAM,

CZUWAM

PIERWSZA POLSKA MSZA SWIETA W ARCHIDIECEZJI
OKLAHOMSKIEJ,ZA PONTYFIKATU OJCA SWIETEGO
PAWLA VI KIEDY ARCYBISKUPEM BYL JOHN R.QUINN
A PROBOSZCZEM PARAFII MATKI BOSKIEJ FATYMSKIEJ
W NICOMA PARK KS,ALOJZY WALECZEK,Z DEDYKACJA
DLA POLAKOW,KTORZY OSIEDLILI SIE W TEJ
ARCHIDIECEZJI.
NICOMA PARK,29-GO GRUDNIA L976

Program from last Polish Christmas mass held in Oklahoma at Nicoma Park, December 29, 1976. Courtesy of the author.

number of families—the Babiaks, Skropkas, Wasiks, and Ocercitys, among others—who were more Polish by association than by actual fact. These people originated in the Russian Ukraine, located near the Czarist sector of Poland. Their speech and social customs blended well with those of the Poles, and until about 1919, so did their religious and political views. Technically they were Orthodox, not Catholic. In their homeland, they had adhered to the Greek-based Ukrainian rite rather than that of Rome. In Bremond, they had found few of their own particular faith and, since they understood Polish, had blended into the Roman Church.

Immediately after World War I, a split developed between these people and the Polish majority at St. Teresa's. According to one version, Father Suwalski determined that it was time to enforce western orthodoxy on the Orthodox, and thus he told them that they had to convert to the Roman rite.[20] According to another, he engaged in "political activity" of which the Ukrainians wanted no part.[21] Quite possibly this activity related to events in Europe where the Versailles conference was granting Poland's independence from Russia, Germany, and Austria. Whatever the exact cause of the schism, the dissenters withdrew and built their own church, St. Mary's, three miles north of Harrah. In 1926 this group affiliated with the Ukrainian Orthodox Church in the United States. After fires destroyed their buildings in 1923 and 1949, the group moved into Jones, Oklahoma, and constructed its present church in 1950.

Unlike the Ukrainian controversy, however, Father Oraczewski's troubles were entirely his own making. His stay at St. Teresa's was notably brief because the bishop discovered that his credentials for ordination were fraudulent. Banished to the Benedictine monastery at Sacred Heart, near Konawa, Oraczewski plotted secession from the church. When the monks there discovered his plans to form a new church with himself as head, they packed his bags and ordered him away. Later, he did establish a church in Kansas. To show that he held no grudges, he extended membership to the Oklahoma bishop. For his misadventures, Oraczewski earned the nickname the "White Pope."[22]

St. Teresa's major crisis of the period, however, resulted not from controversy, but from fire. On March 13, 1923, the congregation of some 200 people, still almost entirely Polish, was shocked by news of disaster.[23] Smoldering charcoal, left unattended after a funeral, sparked a flame that engulfed the old frame church house. Neighbors sprang into action and rescued a number of religious articles, but the building itself was a total loss.

St. Teresa of Avila Catholic Church at Harrah, Oklahoma, the only Polish parish church in the state. Courtesy of the author.

The fire could hardly have come at a worse time, since parishioners' incomes had plummeted with the price of cotton. Still, the churchmen quickly raised a temporary wooden building. Within two years volunteer workers, using mostly donated materials, erected a permanent, brick church building. This structure stands today as Oklahoma's only Polish-Catholic church.

While Polish spiritual and social life flourished around St. Teresa's, Polish economic life developed a more cityward movement. Even before statehood in 1907, three Poles, John Jorski, Adolph Miller, and Joseph Klimkowski, had started small businesses. The former two operated saloons while the last ran a blacksmith shop. Jorski's establishment, the first Polish-owned operation, prospered for several years before the new state constitution ushered in a half-century of prohibition. This particular dispensary went out of business early, however, when territorial officials claimed that Jorski was selling to Indians in violation of the law. Thereafter, thirsty Poles sent to Kansas for liquor, which came to them directly by train as long as such shipments remained legal. These drinkers then joined thousands of others across the state in operating moonshine stills, hidden in the rural countryside.[24]

After the First World War, a new generation of Polish entrepreneurs opened their doors for business. Pete Senkowski began an undertaking service and, together with John Rychlec, a grocery store. Adam Nowakowski set up a barber shop. Throughout the small business district, in fact, signs appeared everywhere denoting Polish ownership of Jorski's Chevrolet dealership, Jorski's feed store, Drzewiecke's grocery, Steciak's blacksmith shop, and Marshall's grocery.[25]

Other Polish young people left their parents' farms to work at Harrah's two cotton gins and cannery and at the Oklahoma Gas and Electric Company's generating station north of town. Sometimes these individuals attained supervisory positions. Robert Wozniak, for example, became head manager of one of the gins. More often, however, these establishments treated their employees less kindly. Selena Kusek, as a fifteen-year-old girl about 1905, worked in the cannery for three cents an hour. A generation later, her son Frank earned only 35 cents an hour at one of the cotton gins. In a reminder of earlier times, one of the Marzecs changed his name to Marshall in order to sidestep alleged anti-Polish prejudice in the personnel department of the Oklahoma Gas and Electric Company.[26]

Despite such difficulties, Harrah's Polish community drifted steadily toward the mainstream of American life. St. Teresa's had no parochial school before 1938, and thus the Polish youngsters attended public schools. This allowed the children to learn the English language from their teacher and American classmates. Unfortunately, short school terms, which gave time off for cotton planting and picking, limited the importance of these contacts. The Polish children in particular, missed many school days and often had to leave school for economic reasons before graduation.

Communication in the classroom was no easy matter, and Donna Wyskup of Harrah provided the following story to illustrate this point: "Emily Kubiak . . . [was] among the Polish children who attended Peach Grove School a few miles north of Harrah. None of the children knew any English until they learned it in school. Emily's father taught her to say her name whenever she was asked, 'What is your name?'. The teacher assumed she knew English. Unfortunately Emily gave the same answer to every question she was asked. The Polish children felt disliked by their teacher because she often lost patience with them. This was due to the language problem."[27] Eventually, however, the youngsters overcame such problems and by the time of the First World War most of the Polish people used English as their primary language.[28]

During the war, thirty-five young men from the parish served in the armed forces, while at home other parish members gave their support to Liberty Bond drives and fund-raising efforts for the Red Cross.[29] About this time too, the parish began a tradition of Fourth of July picnics. Even religious holidays took on patriotic trappings. The 1918 celebration of the Feast of Corpus Christi coincided with the American holiday of Memorial Day. The Very Reverend Urban de Hasque followed Father Suwalski's Polish language sermon with an address in English which emphasized the harmony of American patriotism and "true Catholicity."[30]

Regardless of such evidences of Americanization, however, some prejudice remained. The period between the wars was one of great Ku Klux Klan activity in the state. Although Harrah was spared this group's violence, some of their beliefs inevitably reached the community's native population. Roughneck American youth, who once taunted Polish children on their way home from school, grew into adult voters who barred all Catholics from public office in the town. In fact, not until the present decade did the first two Polish Catholics gain elected positions in Harrah. Even then, majority rule denied re-election to school board members Joe Zawisza and Ed Brzozowski.

Whether local prejudices resulted from anti-immigrant sentiments in particular or from anti-Catholicism in general was not clear because for many years Polishness and Catholicism remained almost synonymous in Harrah. Even in modern times the two groups included many of the same people. As late as 1965, in fact, 163 of the parish's 226 families had clearly Polish names while many other families included people of Polish ancestry. Moreover, in recent times a number of St. Teresa's Polish sons and daughters have entered the service of the Church. Beginning with the ordination of Father Eugene Marshall, O.S.B., to the priesthood in 1950, two men and seven women have joined religious communities.[31]

Driving into Harrah on U.S. 62 from Oklahoma City today, the casual observer can still find proof of the area's Polish heritage. In town, several businesses remain under Polish ownership. The Jorski name, for example, still appears on the mill and on an auto repair shop. Seikel's grocery and Wyskup's insurance agency also catch the eye. With a little further investigation, one can discover the recent site of Adam Nowakowski's retail liquor store in addition to Dan Senkowski's beer bar and domino hall and the Steciaks' plumbing and propane supply store. There are a handful of Polish teachers in the community's school system. Unfortunately, however, there are no Polish doctors or lawyers in the city.

Motoring eastward through town, one sees the best evidence of lingering Polish ethnicity on the grounds of St. Teresa's Catholic Church. Along the hill toward the church, parish hall and rectory, there is the graveyard, with its names from the past and recollections of the successful struggles against wilderness, fire, and economic hardship.

Should one arrive in mid-August, he might catch the annual parish picnic where third- and fourth-generation Polish farmers, shop-keepers, and other working people serve large helpings of hospitality along with *kielbasa,* potato salad, and homemade ice cream. One could lean back and listen as Louis Atamanczyk fiddles, Bud Kusek plays a guitar, and Agnes Czerczyk and Emily Kubiak sing traditional Polish folk songs, along with western-swing tunes. He could hear about St. Teresa's current fiddling star, Benny Kubiak, who, following in the footsteps of Anthony Wilkowski, has played with such notables as Bob Wills and Glen Campbell.

Here, then, is Harrah's Polish heritage as it lives on today in the community spirit of St. Teresa's parish. It is a spirit of warmth and openness befitting the label: "Polish-Oklahoman."

Chapter 4

THE SMELTER WORKERS
OF BARTLESVILLE

Fly Point and Skeeter Row on the north, Smelter Town on the east, Frog Hollow on the east and south, Ragtown (or Pruneville) on the south, and Border Town to the west and southwest of "No. 1": these areas marked the boundaries of Polish settlement in early twentieth-century Washington and Osage counties. As a group, they loosely ringed "Nos. 1, 2, and 3," the zinc smelters of the young and industrializing city of Bartlesville, where the vast majority of the Polish men of the two counties worked. Each of these satellite communities had an identity of its own and each commanded a certain neighborhood loyalty.

Bartlesville was simply too large and non-Polish to merit such affection. By 1907 that prosperous and precocious city had reached its adolescence as a typical American town of about 10,000 souls, most of whom were out to achieve fame and fortune. By the early years of this century, Bartlesville had already become an agricultural marketing center where cattle and wheat growers brought their livestock and produce.

Shipping and retailing were only the first chapter in Bartlesville's small-town version of an Horatio Alger success story. At the turn of the century, industry was developing in the northern regions of the old Cherokee nation that surrounded the city. This was a boom time for mineral production as discoveries of coal, lead, zinc, and later oil, brought sudden wealth to companies operating in the northeastern corner of the emerging state. Bartlesville would share in that prosperity, for with the construction of its first zinc smelter in 1907, the city entered the industrial era. By then, Jake Bartles' little crossroads village was the seat of Washington County, a locale with big plans for the future.[1]

By 1907 lead and zinc mining was the major economic enterprise of the Tri-State area where the borders of Kansas, Missouri, and Indian Territory converged. Found in abundance in this region, both metals had proven their worth to industrial consumers, with zinc in particular already a highly-prized addition to iron and steel making. Producers of these materials had discovered zinc's value as a protective agent against rust and corrosion, and begun coating their own products with it.[2]

The richest of these mineral deposits lay in Indian Territory in an area east of the Grand River and north of the Cherokee capital at Tahlequah. This region, which included Ottawa, Delaware, and parts of Adair and Cherokee counties, would one day make Oklahoma the nation's leading zinc-producing and fourth leading lead-producing state.[3]

Although coal was the traditional fuel for zinc smelting, producers soon learned that natural gas, which burned at a more desirable, lower temperature, could supply their needs more cheaply. With the development of the Neodesha oil and gas field in 1892, zinc smelters suddenly popped up all over southeastern Kansas and northeastern Oklahoma. Collinsville, Oklahoma, at one time had the largest single smelter in the world. But Iola, Kansas, became the country's biggest producer of zinc slabs, called "spelter." Outside of Iola, however, the city which took best advantage of the zinc boom was Bartlesville.[4]

Located near fresh running water from the Caney River and Butler and Sand creeks, Bartlesville was ideally situated for the production of zinc. Serviced by two major western rail lines, the city was only 65 miles west of the Miami mines and even closer to a major gas field, opened just over the Osage border in 1896. By December 1907, the Lanyon-Starr (No. 1); Bartlesville Zinc (No. 2); and National Zinc (No. 3) had all begun operations southwest of the city.[5]

All three companies prospered and by the First World War, they employed some 2,000 men, including many first- and second-generation Polish immigrants recruited from the older smelting communities to the north. In 1906, the Lanyon-Starr Company put labor scouts into the field to round up veteran zinc workers, Poles, Germans, Lithuanians and others, and transport them to Bartlesville. Late in that year, workingmen in such places as La Harpe, Gas City, Iola, Neodesha, Dearing, and Caney in Kansas, began to see recruitment handbills and hear stories about the new plants going up in Oklahoma. The news spread quickly, mostly by word of mouth. Soon

48

MAP 6

Zinc Industry of Oklahoma, 1907 - 1920

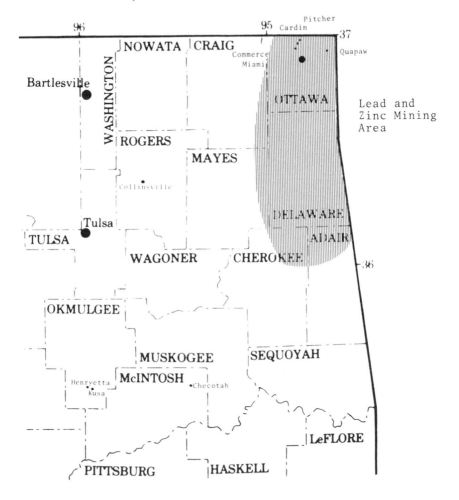

Source: Charles N. Gould, Geography of Oklahoma (Ardmore
Okla., 1909), Fig. 72, p. 127.

people with names such as Polaski, Orloski, Rybka, and Groszek began to appear at the Lanyon-Starr building site, hoping to find jobs inside the new structure. By the time zinc production reached its prime during wartime, there were probably more Poles on hand than there were members of any other nationality.[6]

Valentine Kazmierzak and his son Joe were typical of the working men who migrated to the area during the first decade of smelting operations. Valentine, so-named because of his birth on St. Valentine's Day in 1838, was a native of Poznan (probably the village of Dachowa Kurnick) in German-controlled Poland. As a subject of the Kaiser, he had been eligible for military conscription, and, against his will, had fought on the side of his German masters in successive wars against Denmark, Austria, and France between 1864 and 1870. After the Franco-Prussian war he returned home in good physical condition but with no great love for Chancellor Bismarck and his aggressive designs for a German empire.[7]

Valentine and Jadwiga ("Hattie") Kazmierzak had several daughters, including Victoria Kazmierzak Bartoski, but only the one son Joe, who was born in 1873 after his father's military days had ended. By the time young Joe reached fifteen, Valentine worried that he too would have to serve as "cannon fodder" for the Prussian army or navy. Knowing that within three years' time Joe would start military training, he wrote to Victoria and her husband in Pittsburg, Kansas, for help. They sent steamship tickets for Valentine and Joe, and in 1888 the father and son sailed for America, leaving behind Mrs. Kazmierzak and two daughters who would join them soon.

Joe and his father found work in the newly emerging smeltering industry of southeastern Kansas. After a short stay in Pittsburg, the family moved first to Iola and then to Caney. By the time he was in his late twenties, Joe felt he could support a wife and family of his own. On May 9, 1900, he married Mary Elizabeth Almasy at St. Joseph's Church in Humboldt, Kansas. Miss Almasy, a native of Marine, a village in the Austro-Hungarian Empire, had come to Iola earlier that same year to take care of an ailing sister.[8] As was usually the case in immigrant marriages, he was five years older than she. Family responsibilities came quickly for such newlyweds and ten months later the first of their eight children, a daughter named Helen, arrived.

Joe found steady work at one of the smelters in Iola, and there he remained for eleven years. News of better opportunities later sent them to Caney, and from there south to Collinsville, Oklahoma,

Richard M. Bernard

Polish smelter workers in Bartlesville, Oklahoma, ca. 1910. Courtesy of Bartlesville Public Library.

in 1911. Some eight years later the family finally settled in Bartlesville. Joe worked in the zinc smelters there for seven years, until 1925, when he took a job with the Phillips Petroleum Company. He remained with Phillips until his retirement. Longevity ran in the Kazmierzak family. Valentine died at age eighty in Iola; Joe lived until 1956 when he was eighty-three.

In many ways, the experiences of the Kazmierzak family represented those of the other Polish immigrants who came to work in the zinc smelters of Bartlesville. Although most left Poland in order to better themselves economically, many young men fled to avoid being drafted into the Prussian, Russian, or Austrian armed forces. Most came to the Tri-State District because they knew someone there, a friend or relative who sent word of employment opportunities and sometimes included money to cover the cost of transportation. Generally, married couples came first; daughters and sweethearts following afterward. In keeping with the customs of the homeland most young men waited to marry until they felt that they could support a family. Thus they married rather late, a factor that seems to have been the main limitation on the number of children which immigrant couples had. In order to secure work, or better their positions, families moved frequently throughout the district from one smelter town to another until the whole industry went into decline. Then they either left the area entirely or found work in other industries such as steel, automobiles, or oil refining.

In a sense, one could say much the same for all zinc workers since a remarkably large proportion of them were Polish. The Dillingham Commission of 1911 investigated the zinc-smelting industry in order to determine the national origins of its employees. Considering those groups whose members accounted for at least 1 percent of the work force, the commission discovered that nearly 35 percent (496 of 1,423) of all zinc smelter and refinery workers surveyed had been born in Poland.[9] Unfortunately, the commission failed to report their findings by states, but since by that year the industry centered on Iola and Bartlesville, it seems likely that a large part of the Oklahoma work force was Polish either by birth or parentage.

It is difficult to determine just how many Poles came to Bartlesville to work in the zinc business. Some estimates for the good years before and during the First World War range as high as 400 to 500 families. These figures seem realistic if they include those people who stayed only a short while before moving on.[10] The 1917–18 city directory listed the names of only 119 people of Polish extraction. Some of them were family heads, others were single working men and still others were widows and independent working women. Although Bartlesville directories, like their counterparts in other cities, probably undercounted poor and working class immigrants, the steady decline of Polish names still suggests a rather sharp departure of Poles after the war. In succeeding editions, their totals fell to 71 (1919), 39 (1920), and 17 (1922).[11] The U.S. Census seemed to confirm this exodus. It listed 85 and 74 Polish-born people in Washington and Osage counties, respectively, in 1920. A decade later those totals fell to only 45 and 35. Counting these people and their American-born children, however, there could have been as many as 235 first- and second-generation Poles in the Bartlesville area in the latter year.[12]

Naturalization certificate of Polish smelter worker, Joe Kazmierzak. Courtesy of Mr. Joe Kazmierzak.

Regardless of their exact numbers, hundreds of people, both Polish and non-Polish, began pouring into Bartlesville's southwestern corner, looking for jobs and places to live. Foreseeing this influx, and hoping to secure for the city a steady and law-abiding, family-oriented work force, the members of the city's Commercial Club devised a scheme for turning many of these newcomers into instant property owners, each with a stake in the community in the form of his own individual family dwelling. By such means, they hoped to minimize tenancy and the rowdy, boardinghouse conditions that often seemed to prevail wherever single workingmen congregated.

As a group, the club members purchased a ten-acre tract of land just beyond the western edge of the city, about a half-mile north of the initial Lanyon-Starr smelter then under construction. Surveyors divided this property into 50-foot by 125-foot residential lots, and contractors began erecting inexpensive frame homes. Although equal in size and priced at $100 each, some of these lots were necessarily more desirable than others. One, for example, had a tank house already in place. Another included a producing oil well that would guarantee its owner an outside income of $12 to $15 a month in royalties.

Since the object in building the homes was not immediate profit but rather the attraction of working-class families, it made no sense to auction off the new properties to the highest bidders. Instead, the Commercial Club reverted to one of the traditional means of land distribution in the new territory—a lottery. On December 24, 1906, the club held a drawing and assigned lots on the basis of chance, just in time for dozens of families to celebrate Christmas on their own property.

This initial ten-acre parcel of land became known as Fly Point and Mosquito (or more commonly, Skeeter) Row. Fly Point was located on high ground; Skeeter Row was in a swamp three blocks to the east. These places presumably took their names from the presence of flying insects in homes that lacked door and window screens. The other colorfully labeled areas where the smelter workers lived also owed their establishment to similar moves by commercial and industrial leaders.[13]

The availability of property in these areas, however, implied no guarantee of quality housing. In fact, a great many workingmen and their families had to resort to tents or tar paper shacks for shelter. Lumber and other building materials were in short supply, and their prices were far beyond these people's reach. Desperate for protection from the elements, many of the workers built their homes, using a unique source of materials. Zinc ore arrived at the new plants in railroad cars fitted with interior wooden frames which were, in fact, four-by-eight-foot boxes. Called "grain boards" in farming areas, these rough containers prevented the cargo from shifting through cracks as the train bounced along to its destination. The workmen, however, quickly realized that if a dozen of these boxes stood clustered on their ends, they could form a modest house. Thus the men carried them back to their families who added tar paper to the outside and newspaper to the inside. The former, aided by banks of dirt, kept out the wind and rain while the latter served as wallpaper. In the early years, a great many people lived in these floorless structures, appropriately called "ad hocs."[14]

MAP 7

Smelter Town
1908-20
As Located on a Map
of Modern Bartlesville

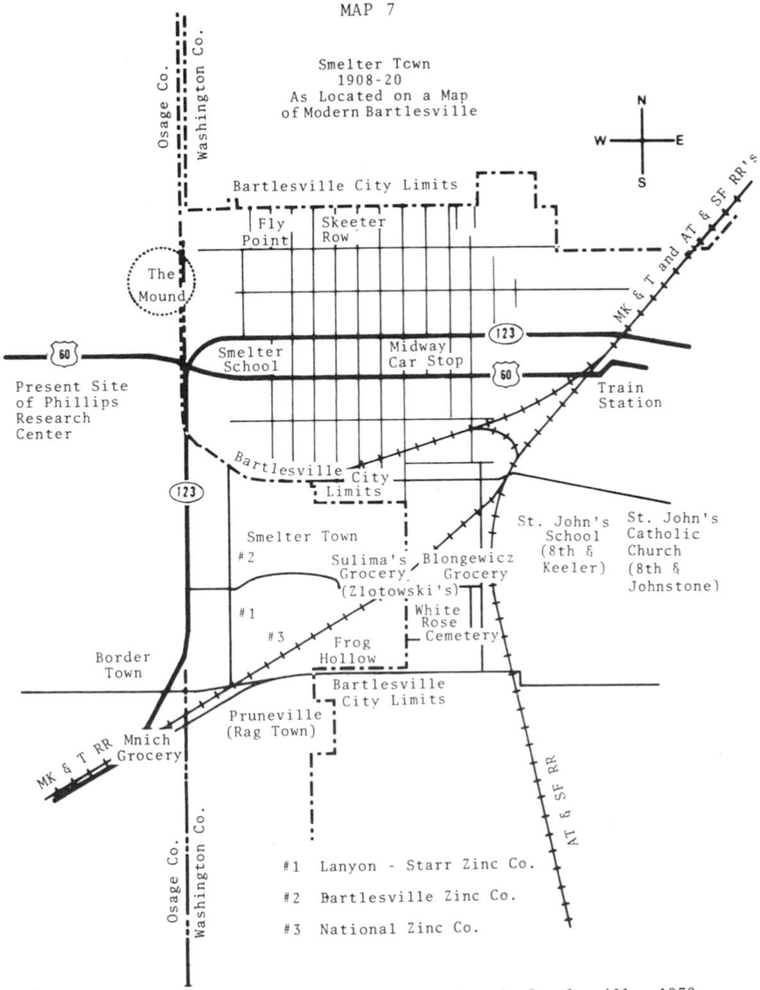

N
W — E
S

Osage Co.
Washington Co.

Bartlesville City Limits

MK & T and AT & SF RR's

Fly
Point

Skeeter
Row

The
Mound

Smelter
School

Midway
Car Stop

123

60

60

Present Site
of Phillips
Research
Center

Train
Station

123

Bartlesville City
Limits

Smelter Town
#2

St. John's
School
(8th &
Keeler)

St. John's
Catholic
Church
(8th &
Johnstone)

Sulima's
Grocery
(Zlotowski's)

Blongewicz
Grocery

#1

White
Rose
Cemetery

#3

Frog
Hollow

Border
Town

Bartlesville
City Limits

MK & T RR
Mnich
Grocery

Pruneville
(Rag Town)

AT & SF RR

Osage Co.
Washington Co.

#1 Lanyon - Starr Zinc Co.

#2 Bartlesville Zinc Co.

#3 National Zinc Co.

Sources: Mr. Joe Barber and Mr. Stanley Kazmierzak, Bartlesville, 1979.

For many years these areas remained the focal points of Polish social life in Bartlesville, more so in fact than St. John's Roman Catholic Church. Many of these Polish people were every bit as religious as their countrymen in Harrah. But, as in the case of the coal miners in the McAlester district, geography and social diversity combined to limit Polish participation in the life of the local parish. Built in 1903–1904, before the coming of the smelters, St. John's was located then, as now, at the corner of Eighth and Johnstone, just south of downtown, but a mile or more away from the homes of most of its Polish parishioners. Moreover, unlike the situation in Harrah where almost the entire parish was Polish, Bartlesville's Poles probably never accounted for more than one-fifth of St. John's adherents. Then, too, it probably did not help matters that one of the few Polish priests to serve there in the early years seems to have been the erratic Father Adam Oraczewski, the "White Pope." The Polish people of Bartlesville, therefore, tended to turn to their own families and neighborhoods for recreational activities and social meeting points.

Aside from the sort of neighborly visiting and family discussions seen elsewhere, much of the social life enjoyed by Bartlesville's Poles centered on common gathering spots, commercial establishments where housewives, children, or workingmen gathered to discuss the day's events. Women, for example, frequently met at grocery stores and meat counters. At first nearly everyone shopped at the Smelter Store at the west end of Third Street (now Frank Phillips Boulevard). The three smelting firms owned and operated this establishment as a partnership in an attempt to regain some of the money paid out to their employees. The store offered its customers convenience, if not bargain prices. On the eve of World War I, however, the Smelter Store burned down while at about the same time a number of Polish-owned markets were opening for business. During the war years housewives could buy produce, and sometimes meat, from: Felix and Estella Blongewicz, Peter and Dora Depalski, Gus and Mary Mnich, Jacob and Frances Sligel, or from Pete Zlotowski and his partners at the grocery bearing his name. After the war when smeltering declined, most of these businesses folded, but some new ones did appear. Polish shoppers could still look to Paniucki and Safranki's, Joseph and Mary Sulima's, or Maurice and Rose Schalski's, among others which came and went, for *kielbasa* and other ingredients for Old World dishes.[15]

Among these groceries, Gus Mnich's has enjoyed the greatest

longevity. Konstanty (Gus) Mnich, a native of Blazowa, Poland, came to Bartlesville in 1908 from Neodesha, Kansas, where he had worked in a zinc smelter. Upon his arrival he found several old friends from Blazowa, who had already settled in the community. On this first visit, Mnich worked at smelter "No. 1," but he remained only a year or two before striking out for St. Louis where he married in 1914. Determined to find steady work in Oklahoma he and his wife Mary returned to Bartlesville where Gus re-entered the smelter.[16] Sensing a chance to move ahead in life in 1916, he pooled his funds with two other Polish men, Loddie Mnich and Henyrk Rybka and built a small grocery just southwest of "No. 1." The partners opened their doors for business immediately, and within a year's time, Gus Mnich became the sole proprietor of the establishment. "[Some of] the Polish people who came to work at the smelter would build sheds to live in," he later recalled. "I built a shed too and started my business."[17] Mnich continued to operate the grocery until he retired, aided by Mary until her death, and after 1929 by his second wife Angela Piotrowski Mnich. Although Gus Mnich died on April 13, 1978, his sons, Tony and Mike, continue to operate the business at its new location opposite the Phillips Petroleum Research Laboratories.

Children might drop by at Mnich's but they were more inclined to spend their after-school hours at Pat's Grocery. Located at the end of the trolley line in Smelter Town, the combination restaurant and grocery owned by Irishman Pat Kennedy was a favorite of the little ones who lived around the smelters. Youngsters would run to Pat's to spend their pennies in an era when a mere one cent entitled a child to order Pat to "mix them up" before he put their candies into a sack.[18]

Single workingmen, on the other hand, came together at the boarding houses where many of them lived and took their meals. Although the predominate form of architecture in Smelter Town was the modest, single-family dwelling, there were several of these rooming houses within walking distance of the plants. One of the most popular was the "Beanery," operated by Mr. and Mrs. Robert Burk, a quite large structure found near Skeeter Row. Such buildings became the sites for many nocturnal discussions and more than an occasional sip of bootlegged liquor.

The men did not have to go far to find alcohol for sale in the legally dry Sooner State. In Ragtown, in addition to several respectable establishments, were some of Washington and Osage counties' best liquor suppliers. These men, many of whom had worked in the mines of Kansas and Missouri before turning to more profitable and less-taxed endeavors, knew their clientele well. Many producers offered a highly popular prune-based liquor whose sales eventually caused a change in the name of the whole area. After state prohibition authorities raided a couple of the local dispensaries, Bartlesville residents began referring to Ragtown by the "high-class" label of "Pruneville," a name that soon became a permanent part of the local parlance.[19]

Grocers, restaurateurs, barbers, feed salesmen, and liquor dealers were not enough however. For clothing and furniture, for education and mass entertainment, Polish people had to look beyond their own neighborhoods and to the American society in town. Sometimes, one simply had to go into Bartlesville. In the days before there were many automobiles, a trip to town meant either walking or taking the streetcar.

The city's electric rail system, which provided the only convenient link between the outlying smelter communities and the downtown business district, was focused on Second and Third Streets. Just as the two interstate railroad lines connected the city with distant suppliers and markets, the Bartlesville Interurban Railway brought smelter workers and their families in touch with schools and businesses nearer to downtown. In the early years of smelter operations, trolleys, running on a spur extended from the main Bartlesville-Dewey line, brought prim and proper Yankee schoolteachers to educate the workers' children. Teachers from Bartlesville high school also came to teach the English language, along with American folkways, to the adult men and women in the immigrant community. In 1913, however, the opening of St. John's School, located a block west of the church, reversed this educational flow. Most Catholic children then paid their round-trip nickel fares, and rode the interurban to St. John's. When school was not in session, some children still rode the streetcar regularly in their roles as messenger boys for businessmen who had yet to obtain telephone service.

One of the young instructors hired to encourage Americanization among the zinc workers was himself a Polish-American named Frank Balcer. Educated at Tulsa University and the University of Oklahoma, Balcer taught history and coached at Bartlesville High School and later at Dewey. He was also a pretty good boxer, though not as talented in that sport as many of his local admirers believed. After an embarrassing defeat by a smaller Texas fighter in 1922, Balcer left for Detroit, Michigan, where he continued his teaching and coaching career. Moved by German and Russian threats to the Polish homeland, he later sailed for Europe and served as an officer in the Polish Army. After World War II, he returned to his adopted city and retired.[20]

The streetcars meant more than educational opportunity, for they took smelter families to downtown stores as well as schools. On the rare occasion when a Polish couple had to purchase ready-made clothing, perhaps a Sunday suit for the man of the house, they rode the trolley to the Zofness Brothers Clothing Store. They traded with Martin I. Zofness at least in part because he spoke their language. A Lithuanian refugee from the terrible anti-Jewish Russian pogroms of 1906, Zofness had come first to Clinton and then to Bartlesville in 1910. In the course of trying on suit coats, Zofness might tell them how he had arrived alone and spotted Joe Kazmierzak, whom he correctly guessed was Polish, and how he startled Kazmierzak with a greeting in the Polish language.[21]

On Saturday nights, however, the streetcars became the province of single workingmen who journeyed into town in search of entertainment. These young rakes sought out the noisy pleasures of ragtime and the dime-a-dance girls who worked at the outdoor dance platform, on the present site of the Phillips Building. Others of them flocked into the movie theater on Dewey Avenue to see what "it" was that such vamps of the silver screen as Theda Bara had to offer. Sunday afternoons were for baseball, but the Saturday night sport was boxing. If no professional match was available, the more rambunctious might engage in their own impromptu affairs.

For some of these men, Monday came all too soon. Beginning in 1908, company whistles blew each morning at 4:00 to announce the start of another working day, and soon thereafter, the firms added 3:00 whistles as well to be sure that their employees were up early enough to get to work on time. There was little excitement or enthusiasm at such hours as the men trudged off to their arduous tasks. Although the work load in the smelters eventually lessened, it was never very pleasant. At best, the whistles called them to hot, sweaty, back-breaking jobs. At worst, they signaled the return to daily danger and possible injury or death.[22]

Zinc ore, when it arrived from Commerce or Miami, Oklahoma, was not really that, but rather a compound mixture of zinc sulfide, silica, lead, and traces of other elements. The central task was to separate the pure zinc by means of high-temperature chemical reac-

tions. The main jobs of the "smelterboys" were transporting the ore and cleaning and preparing the equipment used. This meant long, hot hours of manual labor. For many years after the smelters opened, employees put in twelve-hour days, one crew on and one crew off, seven days a week. Only later did the National Recovery Administration (NRA) pressure companies to shorten the workday to ten, then eight hours, and the work week to six, and later five days. In earlier times, crews sped up operations early in the day in order to finish their tasks near the furnaces before the heat of the sun could make their work unbearable. Such frantic activity often caused men to collapse from heat prostration.[23]

From the workers' perspective, however, life was not so bad. At least they had jobs. Even if they sometimes had to eat their sandwiches while they worked and carry blocks of ice with them to their work areas, they at least had food and places to work. Besides, many of them reasoned, theirs was the best fate possible for men who lacked American schooling. Others held out hope of moving up in the world and eventually leaving the smelters behind.

Such attitudes among the Poles and others helped to explain why unions failed in their organizing attempts. One aborted non-

Richard M. Bernard

The National Zinc Company works in Bartlesville, Oklahoma, 1909. Courtesy of Bartlesville Public Library.

union walkout in 1911 probably soured many workers' taste for collective action. In protest against postwar cutbacks, most workers left their jobs for seven months in 1921–22, but even then they lost. The first permanent union, the United Mine Workers, did not appear until 1933, long after most Poles had left the area.[24]

Shortly after World War I, the Oklahoma zinc industry suffered a sharp decline in activity. After the 1921–22 strikes, only National Zinc reopened for business, and it operated on a greatly reduced scale. Most of the nearby Tri-State District mines had played out, forcing National to buy and transport ore from distant sources. National held on until 1974, however, when it sold its facilities to the New York–based Englehard Minerals and Chemicals Corporation.[25]

What became of the sturdy Polish workmen of an earlier era? For most of them, there was no dramatic answer to that question. As the zinc business began to falter, they simply drifted away in search of unskilled jobs elsewhere. Some migrated to the industrial areas of the Midwest and Northeast where they had friends and relatives in the major Polish communities there. Others moved to

61

Tulsa and Oklahoma City where they blended into the populations of those areas, leaving little trace of their Polish heritage.

Many of the smelter employees and their families, unfortunately, had no chance for future plans at all. They became victims of the massive Spanish influenza epidemic which swept Europe and the United States after World War I. Brought home by the doughboys in 1918 and 1919, the flu virus killed thousands of Americans, many more than had died in the war itself. In Bartlesville it struck the "smelterboys" very hard. One long-time Bartlesville resident recalls that in one week, forty residents of Frog Hollow died—this at a time when there were but thirty homes in that neighborhood.[26] Where flu went, pneumonia followed, and in the days before penicillin, death came right behind. Town officials converted available space in church and school basements into makeshift hospitals, with eight, twelve, twenty beds jammed together under quarantine. Still they died by the score. Joe Kazmierzak's son, Stanley, then a boy of seventeen, recalled the machine-like efficiency with which death struck: "I wheeled them in from ambulances and put the sheet over them, and I wheeled them out the back door." Dozens of Polish people died with the rest. Said Kazmierzak, "I vividly remember that incident because I had never thought about death before until I saw it all there."[27]

A number of Polish people, however, survived the ravages of the flu epidemic and remained in Bartlesville for the rest of their lives. A handful went into business, the most notable being the grocers, Gus Mnich and Joseph Sulima. Like Mnich, Sulima was a native of Poland who came to Bartlesville during World War I. Shortly after the war, he purchased the Three Star Grocery at Eleventh and Rogers. Later he bought a second store at Eleventh and Jennings which he and his family operated until his death in 1946.[28]

Others, most of them second- and third-generation Poles, blended into the occupational structure of the small city. Some, such as Karol Ustrzyski, who became a forty-year veteran of the smelters, stayed on with National Zinc while others found jobs at Phillips. Some worked their ways up to managerial positions; some found jobs as mechanics and workmen. By the time of World War II, it was very difficult to distinguish the Polish from any other white group in terms of their places of employment. For example, Joe Kazmierzak's sons, Stanley and Stephen, each worked for Phillips for over forty years. Stanley's daughter, Linda Simmons, became the director of the Head Start Child Development Center in Stillwater. His son David, an accomplished violinist, became the associate concertmaster of the New Orleans Symphony Orchestra.[29] While the Kazmierzaks were not typical of all of Bartlesville's Polish people, they demonstrated the ability of the city's immigrant workers to move up in the ranks of American society.

The story of Bartlesville's Polish people, therefore, parallels the story of industrial development in that northeastern Oklahoma city. It too is a tale of hard work and individual struggles to make ends meet and to provide for a brighter future. Here, as elsewhere in Oklahoma's Polonia, the emphasis was on family and community, if somewhat less on religious life. Here too, moreover, the heritage is a proud one of survival against odds which were once stacked heavily against the working people of Pruneville and Skeeter Row.

Chapter 5

THE REFUGEE PRIESTS

Number 31216! The only way to identify him in 1942 was by this five-digit figure sewed on his striped, pajama-like camp uniform. This number and a red triangle below it, with the letter *P* in the center marked Father Kasimir Krutkowski as a political prisoner of the Third Reich and an internee at Dachau, one of Nazi Germany's most notorious concentration camps. His story, along with those of a number of other refugee priests, is a fascinating aspect of Polish immigration to the Sooner State. Surely, few other newcomers suffered more themselves or helped more to relieve the suffering of others along the way than did these men.

The Reverend Kasimir Krutkowski, called "Casey" by his fellow priests, had never planned to be a hero. A short man, perhaps under five feet in height, with sturdy shoulders, Krutkowski had been born near Warsaw, Poland, March 14, 1903. Ordained as a priest on Christmas Day in 1929, he settled down to the simple life of a parish schoolteacher. Within less than five years, however, the rise of Adolph Hitler to power in neighboring Germany forced him to change his plans.[1] Fearing the fateful confrontation that lay ahead, Poland began to mobilize its armed forces in the mid-1930s, and among those called to service was Father Krutkowski. By July 1934 he was wearing the uniform of an army chaplain.

In 1939 while retreating with his unit over the nine-mile terrain between Lomianiki and Warsaw, Father Krutkowski saw and heard the horrors of war firsthand as German artillery shells exploded all around him. One came too close. It knocked him unconscious and caused his comrades to leave him for dead. "When I awoke," he later recalled, "there were many, many soldiers running past me towards Warsaw. I ran with them. I ran in the ditch and there were machine-gun bullets flying over my head. Many were killed. I was thanking God I was so short."[2] Eventually, however, Nazi troops overran the area and eliminated all hopes of sanctuary. Father Krutkowski and a friend sought refuge in a small barn, but before they could pry loose enough boards to sneak inside, a German soldier spotted and captured them.

From that late September day in 1939 to April 29, 1945, Kasimir Krutkowski remained a prisoner of war. In April of 1940 his captors sent him to an officers' detention camp at Buchenwald. In late 1942 they transferred him to Dachau, just north of the Bavarian city of Munich from whence Hitler had risen to power. There, during a twelve-year period, over 220,000 people died, including 2,720 religious leaders. Only about 1,700 people, including Father Krutkowski, survived.

Upon his arrival, the prison guards herded Krutkowski and the other Polish priests into Barracks No. 28 and No. 39, separating them from both laymen and the German clerics who were assigned to another building.[3] Among those Polish priests were a number of Capuchins, including Fathers Robert Dabrowski and Wenceslaus Karas, who, like Father Krutkowski, would later make their ways to Oklahoma.

Father Dabrowski had not served in the regular army, but he and his blood brother, Father Hyacinth Dabrowski, did belong to the resistance movement which fought on after Poland's surrender. In 1940, when he was arrested along with twenty-five other priests and brothers, the twenty-nine-year-old Dabrowski held a chaplain's post in the Polish Underground Armed Forces. Singled out as possible troublemakers because of their literacy and previous leadership roles, priests such as he had little chance of avoiding internment and execution. Five months after his arrest, Father Dabrowski fell victim to a Nazi plan to isolate religious prisoners, and thus he joined other Polish clerics at Dachau.[4]

Father Karas had not been in military service at all. A native of Lublin, where he had been born in 1912, he completed most of his schooling there and was ordained a priest in 1937. Shortly thereafter he moved to northeast Poland, near the Russian border, to accept a small parish. He was in that area when Hitler and Josef Stalin signed a nonaggression pact, and the Soviet Union invaded and occupied its share of the Polish homeland. Harassment followed. " . . . they investigated us," Karas recalled, "and told us that we were wrong teaching the people religion. We were supposedly teaching them the opiate of the masses." There was nothing that priests such as he could do. The Russians had "guns and everything." So they simply waited.[5]

In 1941 Hitler violated his earlier agreement and attacked Russia, which brought Karas face-to-face with a crueler oppressor. In 1942 he "had a few visits from the German army, German officers. They didn't like this, they didn't like that; this was a prelude for arresting." Two weeks later, in July 1942, the Germans took Karas into custody, and in another few days he was on his way to a prison in Grodno in northern Poland. He was transferred to Dachau in February 1943.

Life in an internment camp was strenuous at best, even for the most physically fit of prisoners. Dachau's inmates rose at 5:00 A.M. With no hope of breakfast, they simply washed and then swallowed their usual hot drink. "It wasn't really coffee or tea, but some kind of surrogate," reported Father Dabrowski. At six o'clock, they marched off to their jobs where they worked nonstop until noon when they stopped to eat thin, watery soup. They finished work at 6:00 P.M. and then faced a lengthy and excruciating roll call, designed to exhaust them. Father Dabrowski continued, "About 8:00 P.M., we got our ration of bread which was about the equivalent of three or four slices of American bread. Then about 9:00 P.M. we went to bed."

Punishment was often rough. The guards once clubbed Father Krutkowski on his face and head for failure to make his bunk properly. They kicked Father Karas so many times that an abscess formed. Others suffered death.

Then there were the medical experiments. Given no choice Krutkowski and Dabrowski became guinea pigs for the scientific tests of the camp's doctors. Attendants injected Father Krutkowski's right leg with phlegmona, a disease which brings on huge boils and gangrene. Out of a group of twelve who were so treated, he was the only survivor. Ironically, typhoid fever saved him. Owing to an outbreak in the camp, the doctors were afraid to return to finish their experiments, and, thus, he had time to recover. Father Dabrowski survived his captors' experiments with malaria.[6]

Other future Oklahoma priests suffered as well at the hands of Poland's dual oppressors. Father Anthony Hodys, for example, experienced the pains of both world wars. A native of Stryj, Poland, the fourteen-year-old Hodys was conscripted into the Russian army in World War I and ordered to dig trenches. Despite his own loyalty, the Russians deported Hodys' father Gabriel to Kiev. After scraping together whatever funds he could find, young Hodys traveled to that Russian city, bribed a guard, and secured his father's release. After the armistice of November 1918, he joined with other Polish patriots and fought the Russian Bolsheviki for six more months before he fell victim to typhoid.[7]

After the war Hodys joined the army as a chaplain, and at the time of the German invasion he held a post at Krakow, some fifty miles from the Czech border. Taken captive, Father Hodys spent nine months in an internment camp in Rumania. There the guards prevented him and other clerics from mixing with other captured soldiers, forcing the priests to hear Holy Week confessions outdoors in the snow and through a barbed-wire fence. In the spring of 1940 Father Hodys escaped. Traveling via Yugoslavia and Rome, he hurried to join the free Polish forces in France. He was with them as they evacuated that country and sailed for England, arriving in time for the Battle of Britain. There he remained throughout the rest of the war, serving as secretary and chancellor to Bishop Joseph Gawlina, Ordinary to the Polish Army.

The Right Reverend Monsignor Antoni F. Chojecki experienced similar dangers. As a young military chaplain, he followed the Polish army as it retreated from the Russians and crossed the Rumanian border. There he and his comrades were captured and interned at a camp near the seaport of Constanza. As a prisoner, he helped an intelligence officer to engineer the escapes of hundreds of men, including some 300 in one night alone. In 1942 he slipped away and traveled to Egypt to join Polish units there. At the end of the war, he set sail for England where he was demobilized.[8]

At least one of Chojecki's students, Father Marek Maszkiewicz, suffered more from the Russians than from the Germans.[9] Born in 1910 in Garwolin, near Warsaw, Maszkiewicz became a priest in 1936 after studying under Chojecki and others at Janow-Podlaski. Although he hoped to gain university training, the war intervened and on August 15, 1939, he said good-by to his parents and sister for the last time and went to join the army as a chaplain.

At Lwow, he survived the successive Russian, German, and Russian invasions by hiding among a group of Resurrectionist Fathers. Once he just missed a chance for repatriation to Garwolin when he left a waiting line long enough to say mass. Instead, with the final Russian occupation, he became a political prisoner. After keeping him a month in a lice-infested "temporary" prison, his captors sent Maszkiewicz to a labor camp in the Soviet Union. There he broke ice and chopped trees, and, when possible, offered pastoral comfort to the other prisoners.[10] This became all the more difficult when

Father Marek Maszkiewicz with soldiers at a tent-covered altar in the Middle East theater during World War II. Courtesy of Father Marek Maszkiewicz.

one of the other internees stole his prayer book and tore it apart for cigarette papers. Maszkiewicz survived in part because a Swedish doctor assigned him to indoor work away from winter temperatures which sometimes reached 50 degrees below zero.

Sentenced to five years labor in a Russian factory, but sent to his transport train unguarded, Father Maszkiewicz escaped in November 1941. For five months through the Russian winter he sought the Polish underground army. With them he escaped from Russian and traveled through Iran, Iraq, Lebanon, Syria, Palestine, and Egypt. In these last two places he encountered Father Chojecki.

From Egypt, Father Maszkiewicz sailed with Polish troops to Italy where he was wounded during the heroic Polish victory at Monte Cassino.[11] Decorated for his bravery, he later also received a medal for his work to improve Polish-Italian relations.[12] After the fighting ended, he joined Father Chojecki and many other Polish soldiers in England where he supervised three camps of displaced persons.

Brother Stanley Kolowski never served time in Dachau or in the Rumanian camps. He had it much worse. He survived four years at the Nazi extermination camp at Auschwitz. "My name is not Kolowski," he once said. "No. That is the name on the record of my birth. On the rolls of the dead at Auschwitz my name is 4,000,000."[13]

When the war began, Kolowski was an "ordinary young friar" at the Capuchin Franciscan monastery near Warsaw, his birthplace. During the occupation, he and his colleagues aided the underground movement by helping a number of Jews to escape the German authorities. The Gestapo eventually became suspicious of their activities and at one point they took a census of the eighteen friars. Later, they returned unexpectedly and this time they counted thirty-seven robed figures. Clearly, the brothers were hiding nineteen strangers among them. The Gestapo never bothered to sort out cleric and layman, Catholic and Jew. They simply arrested all thirty-seven men.

Torture followed. Kolowski was beaten so badly that his body became "a red mass like raw hamburger." He recalled: "They chained our hands behind our backs and lifted us up to hang by a hook on the wall."[14] Although the symbolism could hardly have been intentional, the guards stuck long needles into his body as he hung in mid-air. Later, the Gestapo placed coins in his hands with the edges running across his fingers. Then they struck both hands with a hammer, crunching them into limp masses.

After a mock trial, Brother Kolowski, the other priests, and thousands like them climbed into boxcars—a difficult task with both hands tied in back. Thus, they began their journey to the portals of hell. Four prisoners died en route in Kolowski's overcrowded car. After unloading, they marched through the gates at Auschwitz and read above them the bitterly ironic words, *Arbeit Macht Frei*— "Work makes one free!" How could they have known that the music they heard the camp orchestra play for their arrival was in fact but a funeral march for thousands.[15]

Kolowski and the others, in what came to be a routine, showered in the baths and ran naked through the snow to their bunkhouse. When they arrived, they sometimes found the doors locked. Since the guards found humor in frostbite, they left their victims outdoors. Sometimes they added to the jest by turning water hoses on them so that their bodies literally froze.

Later, the prisoners went to be photographed. This was a painful process in which the guards jammed the internees' heads against a nail sticking out of a wall so that they would not move in their pictures. Then an artist tattooed a number on each of them. Brother Kolowski, for example, still bears the digits "12988" on his left forearm.

There followed untold suffering. The men had to stand at attention for twenty hours at a time. Slight movements brought instant death. Each day they worked in the fields as at Dachau, but at night they suffered the added pain of carrying bricks in each hand as they returned the two or three miles to their barracks. (The bricks went into the construction of new gas chambers.) They existed on bread and water, the former being about 45 percent sawdust. When the hard work and undernourishment eventually took their toll, the prisoners, being of no further use to the Reich, were executed.

Such a time came for brother Kolowski after four years at Auschwitz. Resigned to his fate, he was truly thankful that the end of his suffering was at hand. "I remember getting in line and thinking, 'My God, it's over at last,'" he later related. But it was not to be. As he marched forward, the doors of the gas chamber suddenly slammed shut in his face. The room was full so the guards kicked him and those behind him away. Cheated in life and now ironically cheated from death, he was overcome by but one emotion, disappointment that his misery would continue.

With the end of war drawing near, the Germans began shifting their prisoners to more secure areas. Brother Kolowski moved from Auschwitz to Berlin to Bergen-Belsen and then to Sandvostel, a camp near Bremen. There he was again ticketed for execution at 7:00 P.M. on April 29, 1945, and had it not been for an Oklahoma tank commander, he would have died on schedule.

But at five o'clock that same day, troops from Oklahoma's Forty-fifth Infantry Division, the "Thunderbirds," approached the camp. Unaware of its existence but curious about its long wall, the officer in charge ordered this obstruction destroyed. No one from the Allied side could have been prepared for the sight inside. As the German guards fled, they left behind literally thousands of emaciated bodies, both living and dead. Among the living was Brother Kolowski who then weighed only 68 pounds.[16]

At almost the exact same moment, other Oklahomans, part of the 157th Regiment of the Forty-fifth Division, rode through the gates at Dachau, where Fathers Krutkowski, Dabrowski, and Karas were still held. Here, too, the Thunderbirds were just in time.

Brother Stanley Kolowski, with Dachau identification number tattooed on his arm. Courtesy of *Poughkeepsie Journal.*

According to a telegram discovered by another priest working in the office of the camp commander, Himmler had ordered that no witnesses remain alive to greet the Allied armies. Eleven guards equipped with machine guns were to open fire on the prisoners from the camp's towers. The Americans arrived less than four hours before the scheduled execution.[17] There were 31,432 people still alive in the camp and all went to their knees in prayer. It was over at last.

After the liberation, Krutowski joined the Second Polish Tank Division in Italy and journeyed with them to England at the end of the war. Dabrowski went to France where the Polish Catholic Mission in Paris gave him the Silver Medal of Merit for Church and Country for his work with metal and mine workers. From there he went to the Netherlands and helped to demobilize soldiers. Father Karas volunteered for service in several refugee camps, the last of which was at Mannheim.

In the postwar years, these priests and several others from similar backgrounds, came to Oklahoma through the efforts of Bishop Eugene J. McGuinness. On a return trip from Rome in the summer of 1948, Bishop McGuinness stopped in London to recruit pastors for his scattered Oklahoma parishes. While there he chanced to meet Father Hodys in a restaurant. The priest was seeking a new diocese outside his Communist-dominated homeland. Theirs was a good match. Once in Oklahoma, Hodys served for twenty years as chaplain for the Carmelite Sisters at Villa Teresa in Oklahoma City.[18]

That summer Bishop McGuinness invited seven priests to come to the Sooner State, including Father Krutkowski. Krutkowski accepted because, he said, he wanted to work here since "I was liberated by the 45th Division from Oklahoma."[19] After coming to Oklahoma, he served at Poteau, Wagoner, McAlester, Wilburton, and Union City, before his retirement in 1976. He died in July 1978, while on a visit to Poland. There he is buried in the Krutkowski family vault at Kostowiec.[20]

Fathers Chojecki and Maszkiewicz came to Oklahoma at about that same time. Thanks to Bishop McGuinness, their paperwork went swiftly and so they arrived in December 1948. They had "expected Indians coming with arrows," but found instead the warm cheer of the annual priests' Christmas party in Oklahoma City.[21] The following year Father Alojzy Waleczak and others came as well.[22]

Father Chojecki served as a chaplain at Tulsa's Monte Cassino School for sixteen years while also teaching theology at Benedictine Heights College. Thereafter, "Father Toni" joined the staff of St.

John's Hospital where he has since remained, well past his July 1971 retirement.

Although he became an American citizen in 1959, Father Chojecki never forgot the people of his native land. In the late forties and early fifties he helped to arrange for some 100 displaced Polish families to come to northeastern Oklahoma. These people became farm laborers, picking pecans and doing other agricultural work in rural areas around Tulsa. Unfortunately, the Protestant sponsors of these Catholic refugees found it very difficult to understand and accept the ways of their charges. Tensions grew between sponsor and refugee, between employer and employee, as the Poles discovered that Oklahoma was not the land of milk and honey for farm workers.[23] Within only a few years of their arrival, nearly all of these families departed for new lives in the Polish-American communities of Chicago, New York, and other northern cities.

In the mid-1960s, Father Chojecki, working with the Bishop of Siedlce and the Catholic Charities of Poland, began sending food and medicine to poor people in Siedlce, the priest's home diocese. In 1971, for example, he sent some fifty packages from Oklahoma to Poland, and he traveled to the old country himself, taking along an additional 700 pounds of drugs and clothing. Through his continuing efforts, 85 to 100 people received daily meals. For his work, Father Chojecki earned the highest of Polish honors, being named Knight Commander of the Order Polonia Restituta.[24] In 1963 Pope John XXIII gave him the rank of the Very Reverend Monsignor, then, the following year, Pope Paul VI raised him to the highest level below that of bishop, to a Right Reverend Monsignor Protonotary Apostolic.[25]

Father Maszkiewicz rode the circuit. In the three decades since his arrival in Oklahoma, he has held pastorships at Medford, Tonkawa, Buffalo, Goltry, Fairview, Ringwood, Hinton, and Bristow. He has also served missions at Pond Creek, Blackwell, Shattuck, Carnegie, Binger, and Stroud. Since 1974 he has been chaplain at St. John's Medical Center in Tulsa.[26]

Also among the early arrivals steered to Oklahoma by Bishop McGuinness was a Capuchin named Father Alexius Lechanski, who had also been a prisoner at Dachau. McGuinness offered Father Lechanski his choice of three Oklahoma parishes: St. Anne's in Broken Arrow, Our Lady of Sorrows in Chandler, or St. Mark's in Pryor. The priest accepted the first of these and soon thereafter he came to the Sooner State.[27]

By the end of 1949 Father Lechanski had convinced four other Capuchins to join him in what one of them feared would be "the isolation of the wilderness of Oklahoma."[28] These newcomers were Fathers Robert and Hyacinth Dabrowski, Wenceslaus Karas, and Raphael Nienaltowski. Over the years others joined them: Father Patrick Joseph Wdowiak, Father Bonaventure Stadnik, Father John Salwowski, Father Zachary Ruszkowski, Brother Joseph Dudziec, Brother Stanley Kolowski, Brother Pius Janowski, Father Sigmund Klimowicz, Father Gregory Gongol, Father Benedict Drozdowski, Father Francis Majewski, Brother Anthony Romaniuk, Father James Meszaros, Father John Schug, Brother Richard Van Tine, and Brother Michael Rosell. All but the last four named were held in the Nazi concentration camps at Dachau and Auschwitz.[29]

Since 1956 Father Robert Dabrowski has led this faithful and long-suffering group of men. Prior to his coming to Oklahoma, Father Dabrowski worked as an assistant pastor at St. Stanislaus Bishop and Martyr Church in New York City and there he operated the "Ave Maria Hour" on Long Island's WLIB Radio. For eleven years, he was the superior of all of the Polish Capuchins in the United States, a position which his brother Hyacinth now holds. Today, Father Dabrowski still takes an active role in the parish life as pastor of St. Anne's where he has the aid of Father Karas who is guardian (local Capuchin head) and assistant pastor.[30]

Together, the Capuchins built St. Anne's Parish into one of the finest in the state. Beginning with property having an assessed value of only $4,500 in 1939, they created a complex of buildings with a church, school, parish hall, their own residence, and although it is now gone, a convent for the Felician Sisters who teach in the school.[31] By the early 1970s, St. Anne's facilities which by then included a number of outstanding works of art, had a total worth of over $665,000.[32] And, they were able to achieve this in Broken Arrow, once a Ku Klux Klan stronghold and, until at least the days of John F. Kennedy, a city where Catholicism was hardly welcome.

Asked how his group had been able to raise this phoenix from the plains, Father Dabrowski replied modestly, "We live sparingly." More to the point, the Capuchins maintained a "crushing schedule" of speaking engagements outside of St. Anne's territory. They traveled from Oklahoma to New York, from Texas to Canada in search of funding sources. Most of the money for their building program, in fact, came from Polish Catholics in northern and eastern cities. The priests themselves built buildings, graded roads, drove buses, and did hundreds of other things without help.[33]

All this they accomplished while residing in self-imposed conditions of alarming poverty. For a while, they lived in the substandard "haunted house" of a Tulsa cleric. Then, after purchase of farm property adjoining the parish grounds, they moved into a rat-infested barn and later into the ramshackle farmhouse where they stayed for two years without the benefit of heat. Their diet was sometimes "not much better than Dachau." Yet, even as they accepted these conditions, these men also donated to the parish the indemnity checks sent to them by the West German government. This fact alone prompted the *Eastern Oklahoma Catholic* newspaper to claim that "the parish was built with the price of their blood."[34]

Perhaps it was their horrible wartime experiences that taught these men, Capuchins and parish priests alike, the special importance of peace, brotherhood, and mutual tolerance which they brought with them to Oklahoma. Once they arrived in the Sooner State, they tried very hard to blend with and serve its people and to adopt its culture as their own. Each morning at St. Anne's, for example, the Capuchins raise an American flag 40 feet above the friary and as it waves in the air, it symbolizes the naturalized status of the fathers and brothers below. Indeed, most, if not all, of the refugee priests who came to Oklahoma became citizens of the United States.

The ecumenicism of these priests, moreover, sometimes extended beyond the tolerance of their parishioners. In racial matters, for example, Father Robert Dabrowski stirred up a hornet's nest when he admitted a Black-Indian girl to St. Anne's kindergarten in 1957. When confronted by angry parents demanding her expulsion, Father Dabrowski may well have remembered the ultimate extent of prejudice he had experienced at Dachau. Said he, "If all our parishioners should leave the congregation because of this incident, and only this little girl and I remain, the one girl—she and I—would be the one, true Catholic Church in Broken Arrow. The Pharisees can leave."[35] On interchurch matters, moreover, Father Dabrowski cooperated in interfaith services held with Oral Roberts University chaplain Robert Stamps. Such services remain rare in Oklahoma.[36]

At work now in their new land, these refugee priests add a proud chapter to the story of Polish immigration. As churchmen, as national heroes, they have brought a new element of pride to Polish-Oklahomans.

AFTERWORD

One hundred and fifteen years passed between the time that Charles Radziminski left Europe for a new life in America and the time that twenty-four-year-old Marian P. Opala made a similar journey yet both came for the same reason. Having opposed their country's enemies, neither wanted to return to a Russian-dominated Poland once the fighting stopped. Both men, moreover, have left their mark on the new land of Oklahoma. One lent his name to a granite peak in the Wichita Mountains. The other places his signature to rulings handed down by the state's highest civil court. Today, the Radziminski name is only a faint memory, but the name of Opala carries weight in every courtroom in the state.

Born in Lodz, Poland, fifty-eight years ago, Marian Opala had no time nor opportunity for the normal path to the judiciary. He was eighteen years of age when Nazi troops stormed into Poland, and for the next six years the battleground was his schoolyard. He served for five years in the Polish underground, and for eight months of that time, he was a prisoner of the Germans. After the war, he faced the prospect of life under a Soviet-controlled Communist regime. In 1949, however, he gained the opportunity to emigrate to the United States under the sponsorship of an Oklahoma family. By the end of the year, he had arrived in the Sooner State.

After earning both a B.A. and a law degree from Oklahoma City University, he worked as an assistant county attorney in Oklahoma County and as a court referee. Thereafter, he became a legal assistant to Oklahoma Supreme Court Justice Rooney McInerney. Along the way, Opala also earned a master's degree in property law from New York University, and in 1977, he won the Herbert Harley Award for Outstanding Achievement in Court Improvement. The following year, Governor David Boren appointed Opala to the state supreme court.[1]

Marian Opala's accomplishment is remarkable, but it is not a solitary achievement. The state's newest congressman, Second District Representative Mike Synar is of Polish descent, the oldest son in a family once awarded a prize as the nation's most "All-American." University of Oklahoma president William S. Banowsky also comes from Polish stock. Frederick Banowsky, his great-great-grandfather, migrated from Poland to Texas in 1848.[2] Similarly, East Central State University president Stanley Wagner is descended from Polish immigrants, as is political activist Jerry Sokolosky.[3] Polish refugee Antoni F. Chojecki's title as a Right Reverend Monsignor Protonotary Apostolic gives him a rank in the Roman Catholic Church just below that of bishop. By any measure, these Polish-Oklahomans are men of prominence and authority who have worked hard to achieve their present statuses.

Hundreds of other Polish-Oklahomans, however, have worked just as hard although the results have been less spectacular. Whether they were miners, farmers, smelter workers, laborers, businessmen, professionals, priests, or laymen, Poles in Oklahoma have always shouldered heavy burdens. They came to the state willing to work to better themselves and their families. Not the best educated and certainly not the wealthiest people to immigrate, the Poles counted on their willingness to work as their hope for the future. That attitude has served them well.

Beyond their belief in hard work, the Polish people of Oklahoma placed great faith in their church and their families. Throughout the country, Poles proved to be one of the most religiously-oriented of all groups. The same was true in Oklahoma where St. Teresa's Church in Harrah stands today as a symbol of that faith. Similarly, Oklahoma's Polish families were very cohesive units who valued home ownership above all other earthly prizes.

Work, faith, and family are the keys to the Polish heritage in Oklahoma. It is a heritage which stresses endurance and survival, not great fame or material wealth. It emphasizes simple religious faith and the warmth of the home in times of trouble. From Radziminski to Opala, the Polish people of Oklahoma have built a strong legacy for their children.

BIBLIOGRAPHICAL ESSAY

A comprehensive history of the Polish people in the United States remains unwritten, but there are several works which cover important aspects of the Polish experience. Victor R. Greene's "Pre-World War I Polish Emigration to the United States: Motives and Statistics," *The Polish Review* 6 (Summer 1961): pp. 45–68, is by far the most thorough on that topic. Joseph A. Wytewal's books, *America's Polish Heritage: A Social History of Poles in America* (Detroit: Endurance Press, 1961) and *Behold, the Polish-Americans* (Detroit: Endurance Press, 1977) are the best available sources on institutional development. Similarly, nothing has ever matched William I. Thomas and Florian Znaniecki's *The Polish Peasant in Europe and America*, 2 vols. (New York: Alfred A. Knopf, 1927) for its coverage of familial and communal relationships in both Poland and the United States. The best discussion of the development of Polish nationalism, however, is in Greene's *For God and Country: The Rise of Polish and Lithuanian Ethnic Consciousness in America, 1860–1910* (Madison: Wisconsin State Historical Society, 1975). No synthesis of the Polish role in American politics has appeared, but one recent publication does juxtapose Polish political activities in several urban areas: Angela T. Pienkos, ed., *Ethnic Populations in Urban America: The Polish Experience in Four Cities* (Chicago: Polish American Historical Association, 1978). Unfortunately, these works say almost nothing about the Poles of Oklahoma, per se.

The history of Polish-Oklahomans remains primarily in the memories of Polish immigrants and their descendants. Thus much of the material used here comes from interviews and letters. These include communications with most of those persons noted in the introduction, including personal interviews (taped and partially transcribed) with: Clementina Gornik, Andrew Waitrovich, Jr., Michalina Sokolosky, Julian and Helen Shamasko, Lillie Bradley and Raymond Hopcus, Selena, Bud, and Frank Kusek, Mary Nowakowski, Father Gerard

Nathe, Hattie Jorski, Stanley Kazmierzak, The Right Reverend Monsignor Antoni F. Chojecki, Father Marek Maszkiewicz, Father Wenceslaus L. Karas, and Father Alojzy Waleczak. Some very limited additional material is available in the *Indian-Pioneer History Manuscripts* of the Oklahoma State Historical Society in Oklahoma City; in the papers of Governor J. B. A. Robertson, which refer to the 1919 coal strike, Oklahoma State Archives, Oklahoma City; in the state mine inspectors' reports, *ibid.*; and, in the coal-company files in the Western History Collections at the University of Oklahoma.

References to Polish-Americans appear in various government documents. Such federal publications include: The U.S. censuses, 1890–1970; U.S. Department of Commerce, Bureau of the Census, *Historical Statistics of the United States: Colonial Times to 1957* (Washington: Government Printing Office, 1961); and *Immigrants and Their Children, 1920: A Study Based on Census Statistics Relative to the Foreign Born and the Native White of Foreign or Mixed Parentage* by Niles Carpenter, Census Monograph VII (Washington: Government Printing Office, 1927); and the Dillingham Commission Report: U.S. Congress, Senate, Immigration Commission, *Reports of the Immigration Commission,* 41 vols., 61st Cong., 2nd and 3rd sess., 1911. Of these, however, only the Dillingham Commission Report deals specifically with Polish-Oklahomans, noting the origins of Harrah's farmers and the conditions of the miners and smelter workers. Specific, if rather limited, material on Oklahoma Poles does appear in U.S. Congress, Senate, Select Committee on Indian Territory, *Report of the Select Committee to Investigate Matters Concerned with Affairs in Indian Territory,* 59th Cong., 2nd sess., 1907; U.S. Department of the Interior, *The Annual Report of the Condition of the Coal Mines in Indian Territory* (1895); and the Federal Writers' Project of Oklahoma, "A Labor History of Oklahoma," (manuscript, Oklahoma State Archives, Okla. City, 1939). Among the published state documents, only the annual reports of the commissioner of labor proved helpful, and even these made no reference to Poles apart from other working immigrants.

There are also varying amounts of information available on Polish-Oklahomans in the following secondary books: Francis Bolek, ed., *Who's Who in Polish America* (New York: Harbinger House, 1943); *St. Teresa* [Harrah], *1925–1975: Golden Anniversary* (Okla. City: n.p., 1975?); Sister Mary Theophane Kalinowski, C.S.S.F., *Felician Sisters in the West* (Ponca City Okla.: Bruce Publishing Co., 1967); Edwin C. McReynolds, *Oklahoma, A History of the*

Sooner State (Norman: University of Oklahoma Press, 1954); H. Wayne Morgan and Anne Hodges Morgan, *Oklahoma, A Bicentennial History* (New York: W. W. Norton, 1977); Frederick Lynn Ryan, *The Rehabilitation of Oklahoma Coal Mining Communities* (Norman: University of Oklahoma Press, 1932); Charles H. Gould, *Geography of Oklahoma* (Ardmore, Okla.: Bunn Brothers, 1909); Margaret Withers Teague, *History of Washington County and Surrounding Area,* 2 vols. (Bartlesville: Bartlesville Historical Commission, 1968); Angie Debo, *Oklahoma: Foot-Loose and Fancy Free* (Norman: University of Oklahoma Press, 1949); Marian Lozinski, *Prze Chodniu Powiedze Polshe . . .* (Krakow, Poland: n.p., 1972); and, Rev. John Schug, *A Parish on the Move: A Silver Jubilee History of St. Anne's Catholic Church, Broken Arrow, Okla.,* (Broken Arrow: n.p., 1973). Similarly, there is material in three important articles: Douglas P. Hale, "European Immigrants in Oklahoma: A Survey," *Chronicles of Oklahoma,* 53 (Summer 1975): pp. 179–203. Stanley F. Radzyminski, "Charles Radziminski, Soldier of Two Continents," *Chronicles of Comanche County,* 4 (Spring 1958): pp. 39–48; and Stanley Clark, "Immigrants in the Choctaw Coal Industry," *Chronicles of Oklahoma,* 33 (Winter, 1955–56): pp. 440–55. Of these books on St. Teresa's Parish, the Felician Sisters and the coal-mining communities, along with the three articles are clearly the most useful for studying Oklahoma's Polish people.

The *Sooner Catholic* and its predecessor, the *Southwest Courier,* proved the most helpful among the state's many newspapers. Beyond these papers, no one source supplied more than a few articles relevant to the Poles. Oklahoma newspapers consulted include: The *Daily Enterprise* and the *Examiner-Enterprise**, both of Bartlesville; the *Broken Arrow Ledger;* the *Daily Oklahoman* of Oklahoma City; the *Eastern Oklahoma Catholic,* the *Tribune* and the *World,* all of Tulsa; the *Hartshorne Sun;* the *Hinton Record;* and the *Indian Citizen* of Atoka.

*This newspaper's name changed several times, sometimes including the city and state in its title.

NOTES

CHAPTER 1

1. Francis Bolek, ed., *Who's Who in Polish America* (New York: Harbinger House, 1943; reprint edition, New York: Arno Press, 1970), p. 370; Stanley F. Radzyminski, "Charles Radziminski, Soldier of Two Continents," *Chronicles of Comanche County* 4 (Spring 1958): pp. 39–48.

2. U.S. Department of Commerce, Bureau of the Census, *Historical Statistics of the United States: Colonial Times to 1957* (Washington: Government Printing Office, 1961), Series C 88–114, pp. 56–57; Series C 171–217, p. 65; and, Series C 218–83, p. 66; Victor R. Greene, "Pre–World War I Polish Emigration to the United States: Motives and Statistics," *The Polish Review* 6 (Summer 1961): pp. 45–68.

3. Greene, "Polish Emigration," pp. 48–49.

4. Paul Fox, *The Poles in America* (New York: George H. Doran Co., 1922), pp. 48–49.

5. U.S. Department of Commerce, Bureau of the Census, *Immigrants and Their Children, 1920: A Study Based on Census Statistics Relative to the Foreign Born and the Native White of Foreign or Mixed Parentage* by Niles Carpenter, Census Monograph VII (Washington: G.P.O., 1927), p. 192.

6. Fox, *Poles,* p. 64

7. Greene, "Polish Emigration," p. 47.

8. *Ibid.,* p. 47–48.

9. Fox, *Poles,* pp. 61–63.

10. Joseph A. Wytrwal, *America's Polish Heritage: A Social History of the Poles in America* (Detroit: Endurance Press, 1961), pp. 61–63.

11. Fox, *Poles,* p. 62; U.S. Department of Commerce, Bureau of the Census, *Thirteenth Census of the United States, 1910: Population,* Vol. I, Table 23, p. 1003.

12. U.S., Congress, Senate, Immigration Commission, *Reports of the Immigration Commission,* Vol. VII: *Immigrants in Industries,* Part I: *Bituminous Coal Mining,* Part IV: "The Bituminous Coal Industry in the Southwest," 61st Cong., 2nd sess., 1911, pp. 10–18.

13. U.S. Department of Commerce, Eleventh Census of the United States, 1890 (manuscripts). Over 90 percent of the nation's manuscript census schedules for 1890 burned in a Washington fire, but a copy of the one for Oklahoma Territory survives at the Oklahoma Historical Society. Children's birthplaces evidence previous places of residence in the U.S. The relationship between Mikolajyagck and the Ambrozes is subject to question. The census lists Mikolajyagck as Joseph Ambroz's father yet given the differences in their names and birthplaces and given Annie's Polish birth,

it seems more likely that Mikolajyagck was her father, not Joseph's. There may well have been others whom the census takers either missed or recorded incorrectly. There were at least twenty-one additional people whom the census listed as born in "Europe" or "Austria" whose names suggest that they may have been Polish.

14. *St. Teresa, 1925–1975: Golden Anniversary* (Okla. City: n.p., 1975?); *Sooner Catholic*, November 16, 1957; U.S. Department of Commerce, Bureau of the Census, Twelfth Census of the United States, 1900 (manuscripts).

15. *Bartlesville Examiner-Enterprise,* March 20, 1966; Martin I. Zofness to Richard M. Bernard, October 2, 1978; interview with Stanley Kazmierzak, Bartlesville, Oklahoma, August 3, 1978.

16. U.S. Department of Commerce, Bureau of the Census, *Fifteenth Census of the United States, 1930: Population,* Vol. III, Part 2, Table 18, pp. 573–4 and *Population: Special Report on Foreign-Born White Families by Country of Birth of Head* (Washington: G.P.O., 1933), Table 14, p. 55 and Table 21, p. 151. The actual percentage of Polish families who lived on farms was 44.8 percent, but another 22.8 percent were classified as "rural non-farm." Some of the "Poles" of the northwestern and southwestern counties may have been Czechs, Germans, or Germans-from-Russia whom census takers mislabeled: Bill Snodgrass to Bernard, Dec. 15, 1978.

17. Correspondence with area residents failed to uncover more than a few Polish families: Jim Olzawski (Okmulgee County) to Bernard, Dec. 26, 1978; Joe Hubbell (Weatherford) to Bernard, Dec. 9, 1978; Georgie Throckmorton (Enid) to Bernard, Jan. 12, 1979; Larry Thorne (Alva) to Bernard, Jan. 11, 1979; Yvette M. Kolstrom (Lawton) to Bernard, Feb. 6, 1979; Snodgrass (Enid) to Bernard.

18. *Special Report,* Table 15, p. 72; Table 16, p. 79; Table 17, p. 92.

19. U.S. Department of Commerce, Bureau of the Census, *Nineteenth Census of the United States, 1970: Population,* Vol. I, Part 38, Oklahoma, Table 49, p. 163; Table 60, p. 184; Table 81, pp. 205–6; Talbe 119, pp. 311–17.

20. Kolstrom to Bernard; Gertrude Kosmoski Sterba (Ponca City) to Bernard, Dec. 17, 1978; Sister Rosemarie, Provincial Secretary, Western Province of the Felician Sisters (Ponca City) to Bernard, Jan. 22, 1979. There were unsuccessful attempts to settle some Polish refugees on farms in Woods County and elsewhere after World War II, but these people did not remain long enough to show up in census figures: Thorne to Bernard.

21. Sister Mary Theophane Kalinowski, C.S.S.F., *Felician Sisters in the West* (Ponca City: Bruce Publishing Co., 1967). pp. 1–23.

22. *Ibid.,* 24–30; Sister Rosemarie to Bernard; and Sister Mary Dolores (Okarche) to Bernard, c. Feb. 14, 1979. Over time, many women from other nationalities also became Felicians, and many of the present-day sisters have Mexican-American origins.

23. Sister Rosemarie to Bernard; *Daily Oklahoman,* September 15, 1975; Mother Mary Liliose and Sister Mary Anilla, "Early History of Felicians Fraught with Many Trials," *Rio Rancho Roadrunner,* c. Dec. 1975. The western province, however, continues to staff St. Philip Neri's, St. Mary's, and Bishop McGuinness High School.

CHAPTER 2

1. Stanley Clark, "Immigrants in the Choctaw Coal Industry," *Chronicles of Oklahoma* 33 (Winter 1955–56): p. 440.

2. Interviews with Mrs. Clementina Gornik, John Daly's daughter, Hartshorne,

Richard M. Bernard

Okla., August 14, 1978, and Mrs. Michalina Sokolosky, Michael Nosock's daughter, McAlester, Okla., August 15, 1978; U.S. Department of the Interior, *The Annual Report of the Condition in the Coal Mines in Indian Territory:* "Accidents Causing Personal Injury or Death in and Around Coal Mines in Indian Territory from June 30, 1894 to June 30, 1895," p. 658.

3. U.S., Congress, Senate, Immigration Commission, *Reports of the Immigration Commission*, Vol. VII: *Immigrants in Industries*, Part I: *Bituminous Coal Mining*, Part IV: "The Bituminous Coal Mining Industry of the Southwest," 61st Cong., 2nd sess., 1911, cited hereafter as "Bit. Coal Indus.," p. 18.

4. Edwin C. McReynolds, *Oklahoma, A History of the Sooner State* (Norman: University of Oklahoma Press, 1954), pp. 266–70; and, H. Wayne Morgan and Anne Hodges Morgan, *Oklahoma, A Bicentennial History* (New York: W.W. Norton, 1977), pp. 151–3.

5. Federal Writers' Project of Oklahoma, "A Labor History of Oklahoma," (manuscript, Oklahoma State Archives, Oklahoma City, 1939) p. 1.

6. S. Clark "Immigrants," p. 442; "Bit. Coal Indus.," pp. 16–17.

7. "Bit. Coal Indus.," pp. 16–19.

8. S. Clark, "Immigrants," p. 443.

9. "Bit. Coal Indus.," p. 18.

10. *Ibid.*, p. 37.

11. Gornik interview.

12. Interview with Andrew Waitrovich, Jr., Hartshorne, Okla., August 14, 1978.

13. Interview with Mr. and Mrs. Julian Shamasko, daughter and son-in-law of Frank Posvkowski, McAlester, Okla., August 15, 1978.

14. Statement by J. G. Puterbaugh, president of the McAlester Fuel Company, to the Oklahoma Coal Strike Commission, November 21, 1919, Papers of Governor J. B. A. Robertson, 8–D–1–1, Box 30, File 13, p. 62, (manuscript, Oklahoma State Archives, Okla. City).

15. S. Clark, "Immigrants," p. 442; Federal Writers' Project, "Labor History," p. 2; Frederick Lynn Ryan, *The Rehabilitation of Oklahoma Coal Mining Communities* (Norman: University of Oklahoma Press, 1932), pp. 27–28.

16. "Bit. Coal Indus.," p. 41.

17. Puterbaugh statement.

18. S. Clark, "Immigrants," p. 451; Waitrovich interview.

19. S. Clark, "Immigrants," p. 451; Ryan, *Rehabilitation*, pp. 29–30; "Bit. Coal Indus.," p. 40.

20. In the nation as a whole, one miner died for each 144,500 tons of coal extracted, but in Indian Territory, the rate was one death for only 73,000 tons produced. The Oklahoma mines were twice as dangerous as those of Kansas and three times those of Arkansas: U.S., Congress, Senate, Select Committee on Indian Territory, *Report of the Select Committee to Investigate Matters Concerned with Affairs in Indian Territory*, 59th Cong., 2nd sess., 1907, p. 69; "Bit Coal Indus.," pp. 68–69; Ryan, *Rehabilitation*, pp. 29–31.

21. Ryan, *Rehabilitation*, p. 30.

22. *Ibid.*, p. 29.

23. Bert S. Tua, "The Immigrant Coal-Miner of Southeastern Oklahoma," (manuscript in the *Indian-Pioneer History Manuscripts*, Oklahoma State Historical Society, Oklahoma City), pp. 8–9.

24. S. Clark, "Immigrants," p. 452; Oklahoma Department of Labor, *2nd Annual Report, 1908–09* (Okla. City: Warden-Ebright Co., 1909), p. 169.

25. "Bit.; Coal Indus.," pp. 42, 48, 62–63. The 675 reporting miners earned an average of $448 for the year while the 48 Poles among them averaged $453. Unfortunately, these are too few people to justify great confidence in the latter figure.

26. Gornik interview.

27. "Bit. Coal Indus.," pp. 64–65; S. Clark, "Immigrants," p. 444.

28. "Bit. Coal Indus.," p. 53; S. Clark, "Immigrants," p. 444. Of the 35 Polish families examined, eleven kept boarders or lodgers who in turn accounted for some 12 percent of the family's earnings.

29. Gornik interview.

30. "Bit. Coal Indus.," pp. 71–72.

31. Shamasko interview.

32. Sokolosky interview.

33. Shamasko interview.

34. Sokolosky and Waitrovich interviews. Polish children sometimes felt harassed in school because of their lack of ability to speak English. Two priests, for example, told the Immigration Commission that Polish children were "dull" and "backward": "Bit. Coal Indus.," pp. 113–4. The sixteen-year-old-requirement became law with statehood in 1907.

35. Gornik interview.

36. Sokolosky interview.

37. *Ibid.*

38. The story of the Carmelite Sisters' attempts to operate schools for miners' children at Hartshorne and Gowen is in *Southwest Courier,* Golden Jubilee issue, October 8, 1955.

39. Ryan, *Rehabilitation,* pp. 29–31 and 34–37; Fed. Writers' Project, "Labor History," p. 2.

40. At least two of the independent stores were groceries owned by Polish people in Hartshorne, the more prominent belonging to Joe Gornik, Bart's son, who ran such businesses from 1922 to 1949: Sokolosky and Gornik interviews; *Hartshorne Sun,* June 16, 1955.

41. Fed. Writers' Project, "Labor History," pp. 6–21 and 62–76; *Indian Citizen* (Atoka), Jan. 3, 1891; *Daily Oklahoman,* June 21, 1894; Ryan, *Rehabilitation,* pp. 45–49 and 62–76; S. Clark, "Immigrants," pp. 453–4.

42. Ryan, *Rehabilitation,* pp. 74–75; conversation with long-time Gowen residents C. G. Fultz and Richard Reed, Gowen, Okla., August 15, 1978.

43. Gornik interview.

CHAPTER 3

1. Charles H. Gould, *Geography of Oklahoma* (Ardmore, Okla.: Bunn Brothers 1909), p. 7.

2. Edwin C. McReynolds, *Oklahoma: A History of the Sooner State* (Norman: University of Oklahoma Press, 1954), pp. 234 and 297–301.

3. U.S., Congress, Senate, Immigration Commission, *Reports of the Immigration Commission,* Vol. XXII: *Immigrants in Industries,* Part 24: "Recent Immigrants in Agriculture," 61st Cong., 3rd sess., 1911, cited hereafter as "Recent Immigrants," pp. 367–70; August Jorski, interviewed by William H. Modrzyski, Harrah, October 5, 1974, Modrzyski, "The Early History of the Polish Community at Harrah," seminar paper, Oklahoma State University, Fall 1974.

4. Joseph J. Janowiak (manuscript account of the early days of St. Teresa's Parish, St. Teresa's Church Records, Harrah, 1929). This composite list originates in two sources with partial confirmation from three others. The former includes the anonymously published *St. Teresa, 1925–1975: Golden Anniversary* (Okla. City: n.p., 1975?), p. 7, and the Andrew Jorski interview as reported by Modrzynski. Mrs. Mary Nowakowski, the ninety-five-year-old daughter of Ike Jezewski, sister of Andrew Jorski and widow of Andrew Nowakowski, confirmed all of the names listed, except Blochowiaks, in an interview in McCloud, Oklahoma, August 14, 1978. Mrs. Nowakowski's younger sister, eighty-nine-year-old Selena Kusek, also verified each of the names listed, in an interview in Harrah, August 13, 1978, as did John L. Hopcus in a letter to Richard M. Bernard, January 22, 1979. Hopcus, however, included Mr. and Mrs. Frank Lutomski and their five children among the original group. The U.S. Census manuscripts for 1900 also confirmed all but the John Jezewskis, Makoskes, and Wozniaks. Modrzynski also found evidence of a Misiah family, but this family has not been verified by a second source. The number of children includes only those born outside of Oklahoma. The author wishes to thank Mr. John L. Hopcus, Harrah, for copying these spellings from the grave stones in St. Teresa's cemetery, Harrah. Even as listed, however, these names and others which follow demonstrate various stages of Anglicizing and several English-language spellings. For example, "Ignatz" had already become "Ike," but "Jezewski" had not yet changed to "Jorski."

5. Quoted in the *Sooner Catholic*, November 16, 1975.

6. Janowiak manuscript.

7. Nowakowski interview.

8. *Sooner Catholic.*

9. Modrzynski paper.

10. Nowakowski interview.

11. Interview with Hattie Jorski, Harrah, August 11, 1978.

12. Frances Kupczynski Magott, daughter-in-law of Apolinary and Mary Magott, story as told to her daughter Mrs. Mary Hopcus, letter from Mary Hopcus to Bernard, January 12, 1979.

13. Nowakowski interview.

14. Interview with Joseph's grandson, Valentine Klimkowski, Harrah, September 29, 1974, as reported by Modrzynski.

15. Interview with Raymond A. Hopcus, Harrah, August 11, 1978; and, "Recent Immigrants," p. 365.

16. U.S., Department of Commerce, Bureau of the Census, Thirteenth Census of the United States, 1910 (manuscripts), handcount courtesy of Prof. Douglas P. Hale, Oklahoma State University, Stillwater. Some of these lands have remained in the same families for three or more generations. Ike Wyskup left his farm to his son Tony, who left it in turn to his son, Frank, who still owns it. Letter from Donna Wyskup to Bernard, January 15, 1979.

17. *St. Teresa, 1925–1975*, pp. 9–10.

18. Nowakowski interview. This marriage and nearly all that followed for many years occurred within the Polish group. Out-marriages were rare.

19. St. Teresa's Parish Records.

20. Modrzynski, paper, presumably based on an interview with Mrs. August Jorski, Harrah, October 5, 1974. Modrzynski, however, mistakenly identified the priest involved as Father Lepich.

21. Father James Murphy, pastor at St. Teresa's, 1955–58, undated notes based

on his conversation with a Father Joseph of St. Mary's, as reported in *St. Teresa, 1925–1975*, pp. 12–14.

22. Interview with Father Gerard Nathe, pastor at St. Teresa's, Harrah, August 13, 1978.

23. Of the 201 names of the parish roll of 1925, 194 were clearly Polish. St. Teresa's Records.

24. Hopcus, interview. Miller's operation is shrouded in conflicting memories. While all agree that he ran a saloon, some say he competed with Jorski, others that he bought out Jorski, and still others that his tavern was in McCloud, not Harrah.

25. Interviews with Hopcus and Mrs. Lillie Bradley, Martin Wozniak's grand-daughter, Harrah, August 13, 1978; Hopcus to Bernard.

26. Interview with Leo "Bud" Kusek, Harrah, August 13, 1978.

27. Wyskup letter.

28. Often this "English" was, in fact a mixture of the two languages. For example, " . . . give me *mlotek* (a hammer)" or "Me monkey (*monka*, or in English, flour) today and you monkey tomorrow" —in other words, "If you will loan me some flour today, I will repay you in kind tomorrow." Magott story.

29. *St. Teresa, 1925–1975*, p. 20. Polish communities throughout the U.S. strongly supported the war effort, for its success brought about a restoration of the Polish homeland.

30. *Orphans' Record* (official newspaper of the diocese of Oklahoma), July 1918.

31. These include: Carmelite Sisters Ann Rudek, Bernadette Zayonc, Imedla Brzozowski, Patricia Kopycinski, Teresa Margaret Layman, and Joan Teresa Korhuniak; Benedictine Sister Seraphia Nickel; and Brother Victor Kopycinski, O.C.D. *St. Teresa, 1925–1975*, p. 23.

CHAPTER 4

1. The best history of the Bartlesville area is Margaret Withers Teague's *History of Washington County and Surrounding Area*, 2 vols. (Bartlesville: Bartlesville Historical Commission, 1968).

2. Edwin C. McReynolds, *Oklahoma: A History of the Sooner State* (Norman: University of Oklahoma Press, 1954), p. 405.

3. Charles N. Gould, *Geography of Oklahoma* (Ardmore, Okla.: Bunn Brothers, 1909), pp. 137–78; and Angie Debo, *Oklahoma: Foot-Loose and Fancy-Free* (Norman: University of Oklahoma Press, 1949), pp. 104–105.

4. *Bartlesville, Oklahoma, Examiner-Enterprise,* February 20, 1975.

5. Information on the establishment of the three smelters comes from: Teague, *History,* Vol. II, 97–110; *Bartlesville Daily Enterprise,* March 10, 1908; Joe Williams, *Bartlesville: Remembrances of Times Past, Reflections of Today* (Bartlesville: IRW REDA Pump Division, 1978).

6. The first Pole in the Bartlesville area may have been Auguste Rowducka, a farmer who appears in the 1860 U.S. Census for the Coo-wee-scoo-wee district of the Cherokee Nation, but nothing else is known of him. J. H. Barber to Richard M. Bernard, April 24, 1979. Although Americans and other immigrants were certainly part of the work force, Poles always appear first in historical accounts, often to the exclusion of all other groups: Teague, *History;* Williams, *Bartlesville;* Bern F. Buff (longtime official of the National Zinc Company) in a speech to the Washington

Richard M. Bernard

County Historical Society as reported by the *Bartlesville Examiner-Enterprise*, March 20, 1966; and Ron Capps (project engineer for the same company) in another speech to the society as reported in the same newspaper February 20, 1975.

7. Interview with Stanley Kazmierzak (grandson of Valentine), Bartlesville, Okla., August 3, 1978, and Kazmierzak's scrapbooks on Poles in Bartlesville, Book No. 2, which he loaned to the author.

8. Marine, in the Austro-Hungarian Empire, became Spisko-Stolica, Czechoslovakia, after World War I, and then Nalepkova, Russia, after World War II. Mary Kazmierzak's citizenship papers listed her in 1942 as Czechoslovakian.

9. U.S., Congress, Senate, Immigration Commission, *Reports of the Immigration Commission*, Vol. VI; *Immigrants in Industries*, Part 21: "Diversified Industries," 61st Cong., 3rd sess., 1911, pp. 39–40.

10. Kazmierzak interview.

11. The number of Poles in the 1923, 1924, and 1925 directories were only 7, 6, and 12, respectively. Mr. Kazmierzak, a long-time Bartlesville resident, went through each directory and identified the Polish names.

12. U.S., Department of Commerce, Bureau of the Census, *Fourteenth Census of the United States, 1920: Population*, Vol. III, Table 12, pp. 827–28; and, *Fifteenth Census, 1930: Population*, Vol. III, Part 2, Tables 18–19, pp. 573–75. Sometimes, the 1910 Poles, entirely omitted as a national group, can be rediscovered by counting persons born in Germany, Austria, or Russia, who spoke Polish as their first language. However, in this case, a private, unpublished tally from the Personal Service Branch of U.S. Census Bureau's Pittsburg, Kansas, office uncovered only thirty Polish men and five Polish women in all of Washington County and none at all in Osage County, even though there was a known cluster of Polish workingmen's homes just west of No. 1., across the Osage County line. Correspondence with James Van Houten, operations officer, U.S., Department of Commerce, Bureau of the Census, Pittsburg, Kansas, 1979, and subsequent telephone conversation, March 5, 1979.

13. Teague, *History*, p. 101. The general area around the smelters assumed the name of "Smelter Town," or to some, "Sin City." Moreover, there was more than one "Skeeter Row" as the name later stuck to homes in swampy areas such as the land below Pruneville.

14. Barber to Bernard. One man even became a real estate developer, in a sense, by constructing and renting these dwellings. His homes, called Blake Row, were on Virginia Street, between Eleventh and Fourteenth streets.

15. Bartlesville city directories, 1917–18, 1919, and 1922.

16. *Bartlesville (Okla.) Examiner-Enterprise*, October 10, 1957.

17. *Tulsa Tribune*, March 23, 1972; *Bartlesville Oklahoma Examiner-Enterprise*, April 13, 1979.

18. *Bartlesville (Okla.) Examiner-Enterprise*, October 10, 1957; Kazmierzak interview.

19. *Bartlesville (Okla.) Examiner-Enterprise, ibid.*

20. *Bartlesville (Okla.) Examiner-Enterprise, ibid;* Kazmierzak Scrapbooks, Book No. 1.

21. Speech by Martin I. Zofness to the Washington County Historical Society, Bartlesville, Okla., April 17, 1974.

22. *Bartlesville (Okla.) Examiner-Enterprise*, October 10, 1957.

23. *Bartlesville Daily Enterprise* March 10, 1908; Kazmierzak interview; Barber to Bernard.

24. Oklahoma Department of Labor, *Fourth Annual Report, 1910–11* (Guthrie

Okla., Leader Print, 1912), 33–34. *Bartlesville (Okla.) Examiner-Enterprise,* October 10, 1957. According to zinc company official, the workers at "No. 3" struck for twenty months after World War I; Barber to Bernard.

25. Teague, *History,* p. 105–6; Williams, *Bartlesville,* p. 53; Buff speech.

26. Barber to Bernard.

27. Kazmierzak interview. One long-time veteran of the smelters, W. L. Morris, Sr., claims that the epidemic took the lives of over half of Bartlesville's Poles, Barber to Bernard. Two Polish men from Bartlesville lost their lives in World War I itself, Anton J. Tyschkewicz and William Yaseck. Tyschkewicz and James H. Teel were the first from Bartlesville to die in the war, and after the war there was an effort to name the newly-formed American Legion Post after both lads. The city's surviving veterans, however, learned that Teel had died first, and thus they named the post for him.

28. Kazmierzak Scrapbooks, Book No. 4.

29. *Ibid.,* Book No. 2.

CHAPTER 5

1. *Sooner Catholic,* April 18, 1976.

2. *Ibid.*

3. Interview with Father Wenceslaus L. Karas, Broken Arrow, Oklahoma, August 17, 1978.

4. *Eastern Oklahoma Catholic,* April 24, 1977. The quotations from Father Dabrowski all originated in this source. See also *Broken Arrow Ledger,* July 21, 1977.

5. Karas interview. The quotations from Father Karas all originated in this interview.

6. Interview with Father Alojzy Waleczak, Nicoma Park, Oklahoma, August 14, 1978; conversation with Father Herman J. Folken, McAlester, Oklahoma, August 15, 1978; *Sooner Catholic* and *Eastern Oklahoma Catholic.*

7. *Sooner Catholic,* June 11, 1978.

8. Interview with the Right Reverend Monsignor Antoni F. Chojecki, Tulsa, Oklahoma, August 17, 1978.

9. Father Marek Maszkiewicz to Richard M. Bernard, November 7, 1973.

10. *The Pulse* of St. John's Medical Center, Tulsa, Oklahoma, June 1974.

11. Maszkiewicz, military discharge papers from the Polish Armed Forces, December 22, 1948. The story of Father Maszkiewicz's role in the Italian campaign appears in a book by his battalion officer: Marian Lozinski, *Prze Chodniu Powiedze Polsche* . . . (Krakow, Poland: n.p., 1972).

12. *The Hinton* (Okla.) *Record,* April 20, 1961.

13. *Poughkeepsie* (New York) *Journal,* April 4, 1971 and *National Catholic Reporter,* April 21, 1978. Unless otherwise noted, the material on Father Kolowski comes from the former source.

14. *Ibid.*

15. CBS-TV, "60 Minutes" program, August 27, 1978.

16. *National Catholic Reporter,* April 21, 1978.

17. Karas interview.

18. Since 1971, Father Hodys has done pastoral work at Gallup, New Mexico; Medford, Okarche, Tonkawa, and Billings, Oklahoma; and in Texas. He now lives at the Center for Christian Renewal in Oklahoma City and still serves as pastor at Mercy Health Center. *Sooner Catholic,* June 11, 1978.

19. *Sooner Catholic,* April 18, 1976.

20. *Eastern Oklahoma Catholic,* August 13, 1978 and *Sooner Catholic,* August 20, 1978.

21. Conversation with Father Marek Maszkiewicz, Tulsa, Oklahoma, August 17, 1978.

22. Father Waleczek was born in southwestern Poland in 1914. Harassed by the Germans, he escaped to England where he met Bishop McGuinness. When he arrived in 1948 or 1949, there were already eight Polish priests in the state. He pastored at Holy Angels Parish in Oklahoma City and at Geary, Watonga, Bison, Newkirk, and Chilocco. Presently, he is in charge of Our Lady of Fatima Church in Nicoma Park, just east of Oklahoma City.

23. Chojecki interview. For example, one employer angrily telephoned Chojecki when one of the married women in his employ became pregnant.

24. *Tulsa World,* June 24, 1971.

25. *The Pulse,* July 1970.

26. Maszkiewicz to Bernard.

27. There are conflicting reports as to where this meeting took place. Father Karas indicated that it was in London, but a recent parish history says New York. See: Reverend John Schug, *A Parish on the Move: A Silver Jubilee History of St. Anne's Catholic Church, Broken Arrow, Okla.* (Broken Arrow, n.p., 1973), p. 3.

28. Father Hyacinth Dabrowski quoted in the *Trenton* (N.J.) *Monitor* April 27, 1978.

29. Of these only two Polish Capuchins, Fathers R. Dabrowski and Karas, remain at St. Anne's Friary. All of the other friars of their province in the U.S., including Brother Kolowski, reside in Oak Ridge, N.J., and work in Polish-speaking American and Eastern Rite Catholic parishes in New Jersey and New York. Father John Schug of St. Anne's has cassette interviews with the fathers of the parish.

30. *Eastern Oklahoma Catholic,* April 24, 1977; Schug, *Parish on the Move,* pp. 21–23.

31. See Chapter One.

32. The Fathers Dabrowski were able to obtain several very valuable paintings and sculptures for a pittance after the war. For example, they rescued Andrychewicz's *Return from Sunday Mass* from a Communist official who thought it worthless. Once restored, its appraised value was $30,000, and even that figure would double if it were in Poland. Schug, *Parish on the Move,* pp. 19–21.

33. *Ibid.,* pp. 2–3.

34. *Eastern Oklahoma Catholic,* April 24, 1977.

35. Reverend John Schug to Dr. John W. McDonald, Broken Arrow, December 19, 1974.

36. There are many less dramatic evidences of assimilation and tolerance. For example, among his other activities, Father Maszkiewicz joined the Blackwell troop of the Boy Scouts of America, the Buffalo chapter of the Lions Club, and the Bristow Rotary Club and Ministerial Alliance, of which he was president. *Record-Citizen* (Bristow), December 11, 1972.

AFTERWORD

1. *Tulsa Tribune,* November 21, 1978.
2. *Bartlesville, Oklahoma, Examiner-Enterprise,* September 14, 1978.
3. Stanley Wagner to Richard M. Bernard, September 14, 1978, and Jerry Sokolosky to Bernard, August 18, 1978.